UNDERSTANDING
Our
JEWISH
NEIGHBORS

ALSO SEE:

Understanding Our Catholic Neighbors
&
Understanding Our Evangelical Neighbors

UNDERSTANDING *Our* JEWISH NEIGHBORS

RABBI MARK S. DIAMOND &
PROFESSOR SHON D. HOPKIN

CFI
An imprint of Cedar Fort, Inc.
Springville, Utah

© 2024 The John A. & Leah D. Widtsoe Foundation
All rights reserved.

No part of this book may be reproduced in any form whatsoever, whether by graphic, visual, electronic, film, microfilm, tape recording, or any other means, without prior written permission of the publisher, except in the case of brief passages embodied in critical reviews and articles.

This is not an official publication of The Church of Jesus Christ of Latter-day Saints. The opinions and views expressed herein belong solely to the author and do not necessarily represent the opinions or views of Cedar Fort, Inc. Permission for the use of sources, graphics, and photos is also solely the responsibility of the author.

Paperback ISBN 13: 978-1-4621-4693-2
eBook ISBN: 978-1-4621-4765-6

Published by CFI an imprint of Cedar Fort, Inc.
2373 W. 700 S., Suite 100, Springville, UT 84663
Distributed by Cedar Fort, Inc., www.cedarfort.com

Library of Congress Cataloging Number: 2024930120

Cover design by Shawnda Craig
Cover design © 2024 Cedar Fort, Inc.

Printed in the United States of America
10 9 8 7 6 5 4 3 2 1
Printed on acid-free paper

To my wonderful wife, children, children-in-law, and grandchildren,
whose love and support sustain me.

To my parents, Frank and Ann Diamond, of blessed memory,
who taught me to understand and appreciate our neighbors.

Rabbi Yohanan ben Zakkai asked his disciples:
"Look about you and tell me, which is the way in life to
which a person should cleave?"
Rabbi Yose answered: "A good neighbor."
(Mishnah Pirkei Avot *2:13)*

—Mark Diamond

To my father, who sang as a soloist in synagogue as a young man,
and to my mother, who motivated me to seek
after all things that are good.
To my wife and children, who challenge and inspire me
to improve each day of my life.

—Shon Hopkin

Contents

Preface ix

Introduction xi

SECTION 1: JEWISH BELIEFS AND DOCTRINES

1. Beginnings of the Jewish Tradition...3
2. Jewish Beliefs and Doctrines 9
3. Beliefs in Common with Latter-day Saints 33
4. Areas Where Latter-day Saint Beliefs Differ.............................47
5. Latter-day Saint "Holy Envy" of Jewish Beliefs........................59

SECTION 2: JEWISH PRACTICES

6. General Overview of Jewish Practices.......................................67
7. Practices in Common with Latter-day Saints 91
8. Areas Where Latter-day Saint Practices Differ 107
9. Latter-day Saint "Holy Envy" of Jewish Practices 119

SECTION 3: INTERFAITH DIALOGUE

10. Latter-day Saint Engagement with Judaism 125
11.. Jewish "Holy Envy" of Latter-day Saint Beliefs and Practices..........135

APPENDICES

Comparison of Jewish and Latter-day Saint Beliefs and Practices 141

Glossary of Jewish Terms 147

Important Figures 159

Suggested Readings 164

About the Authors..167

Preface

The *Understanding Our Neighbors* series is designed to help members of The Church of Jesus Christ of Latter-day Saints become better neighbors and friends with those of other faiths. As the title of this series suggests, our goal is to understand others better so we can stand together with them in matters of faith, support and defend them in times of need, and rejoice in the mutual discovery of deep friendship. Such genuine love, support, and commitment are at the heart of what is often called "interfaith dialogue."

The purpose of the *Understanding Our Neighbors* series is to provide an example of meaningful interfaith dialogue so that Church[1] members can better appreciate the faith and traditions of our neighbors, their commitment to God, and how they seek to honor Him in their lives. Efforts to convert others, no matter how sincere or well-intentioned, are incompatible with this effort to create community understanding and appreciation. While Latter-day Saints often focus on our responsibility to preach the gospel, interfaith dialogue serves a different purpose—it is a meaningful, two-way conversation where both Latter-day Saints and our neighbors of other faiths learn from one another and leave more committed to and excited about their own religion. Having been strengthened spiritually, we can

---

1. In this book, we use the capitalized term "Church" to refer to The Church of Jesus Christ of Latter-day Saints and the lowercase "church" to refer to other faith communities. This differentiation is meant as a sort of shorthand and does not imply that other religious groups are less valuable to God's work in the world.

both find ways to work together in common causes of righteousness and go forth to bless the world in our own unique and inspired ways.

We encourage all people of faith to make every effort to draw closer to God, and hope this series can help each of us to take our religious commitments more seriously, to live holier lives, and to be better religious neighbors.

Introduction

Discovering Judaism for a Christian Restorationist is a journey that feels very familiar. All Latter-day Saints on Sunday morning are used to singing about Israel: "Israel, Israel, God is Calling," "Redeemer of Israel," "Far, Far, Away on Judea's Plains." Our terminology is replete with references to our belief in our status as being of the "House of Israel" and spiritually our patriarchal blessings place us in one of the tribes of Israel.

So, many of the terms are familiar. And, because Latter-day Saints feel a special affinity with the Jewish Holy Scriptures (the "Old Testament") and so much of its teachings, doctrines and practices (temples, the patriarchal order, living prophets, and being a "peculiar people"), we sometimes think we know everything we need to about Jewish traditions, religion, and history.

This wonderful volume will both reinforce some perspectives and change others. It is a treasure trove of both information and insights that will enlarge our understanding of the breadth and intellectual depth of both the religion and the God whom they worship.

Perhaps, it is also needed to say that to refer to the Jewish religion and traditions using "THE", as if there is only one set of beliefs, would be a big mistake. Some of the more well-known branches have been called Hasidic, Conservative, and Reformed Judaism. Culturally, the three main designations based on geographic origin are Ashkenazi, Sephardic, and Mizrahi. Others exist as well.

As a result, we are grateful for this work by scholar Rabbi Mark S. Diamond. But recognize that it is not the only perspective. Rather, it touches on those commonalities that define the Jewish way of observing, practicing,

xi

and thinking that have preserved this great religion through the millennia, and sustained its people and the very legal system they have created as a gift for us all today.

We are also grateful to Dr. Shon D. Hopkin at Brigham Young University who has labored equally to make this understandable to the rest of us, so that as we engage with our Jewish neighbors, we will be sensitive to their ways of observing their beliefs in their daily lives. Hopefully, this will help us be better neighbors.

The Widtsoe Foundation is dedicated to bringing together an understanding of the great religious traditions of the world to help the members of The Church of Jesus Christ of Latter-day Saints be better community citizens . . . and the communities we serve to better understand Latter-day Saints as well. This Understanding Our Neighbors series has been commissioned by the Widtsoe Foundation as one important part in beginning a mutual understanding and appreciation one for another. This volume of Understanding Our Jewish Neighbors will be followed by the third of the three "people of the book" series (Christianity, Judaism and Islam).

Larry L. Eastland, PhD
Chair & President, The John A. & Leah D. Widtsoe Foundation

SECTION 1
Jewish Beliefs and Doctrines

1

Beginnings of the Jewish Tradition

By Rabbi Mark S. Diamond

The origins of the Jewish faith tradition begin with the stories and laws of the Torah, or Five Books of Moses. God's mysterious call to Abram[1] set the patriarch on a journey from Haran to the land of Canaan, then to Egypt, and back to Canaan. According to Jewish tradition, Abram was the first person on earth to uphold monotheism, belief in one God. The Genesis narratives tell us that Abram sealed a *berit*[2] with God and received a new name, Abraham, "father of a multitude of nations." His wife, Sarai, underwent a similar name change and became Sarah, "princess."

The Torah relates that Abraham and Sarah were blessed with Isaac, a son in their old age. The patriarch sent his faithful servant Eliezer to find a suitable wife for Isaac. His mission was fulfilled when Isaac married Rebekah. Thus, the lineage of patriarchs and matriarchs that began with Abraham and Sarah passed on to Isaac and Rebekah, and then on to Jacob and his two wives, Leah and Rachel. The names and images of these seven biblical

---

1. Genesis 12.
2. Covenant. All italicized words are transliterations of Hebrew terms into characters that English-speaking readers can understand. Note that there is no one universally accepted way of rendering Hebrew characters into English ones.

forebears—three patriarchs and four matriarchs—are reverently recited in Jewish liturgical[3] texts to this very day.

One of them achieved a unique status in later Jewish tradition. Like his grandfather Abraham, Jacob received a new name that signified a profound change in his life. After his wrestling match with an angelic adversary,[4] Jacob shed the negative imagery of his given name. *Ya'akov* (Jacob), the baby boy who emerged from his mother's womb clutching the *aykev*[5] of his brother Esau, thus became Israel, the one who persevered with God. The people of Israel (the Jewish people), the Land of Israel, and the modern nation State of Israel all hark back to this ancient story.

The patriarchal and matriarchal stories in the Book of Genesis paint colorful and multifaceted portraits of these biblical characters. They performed acts of deep faith and righteous conduct—opening their own tent to strangers, arguing with God to save the just inhabitants of sinful cities, worshiping one God, and bringing others to their new faith. Nonetheless, they were human beings with moral flaws and faults—passing off their wives as sisters in order to save their own lives, cheating a brother out of his birthright, fooling a father to receive his choicest blessing. Perhaps the timeless beauty and majesty of the Torah lies in the sheer honesty and enduring realism of these stories.

The book of Genesis is first and foremost the history of clans that form the nucleus of a new community of faith. The stories about Joseph introduce the names of sons and grandsons whose descendants would later become the tribes of ancient Israel. In addition, the story of Joseph brings us from Israel to Egypt, where an ex-slave was cast into prison by a jealous master and became the viceroy of a mighty nation and savior of his long-lost brothers and father.

While Genesis is the record of patriarchs, matriarchs, and their families, Exodus is the epic of the birth of a people and a nation. Joseph's descendants were enslaved in Egypt and endured four centuries of forced labor at the hands of Egyptian taskmasters. Pharaoh ordered all Hebrew male children to be killed shortly after birth. One baby, Moses, escaped the royal decree and grew up in the royal household. He fled to the wilderness after witnessing the cruel mistreatment of a Hebrew slave, only to return to Egypt at

---

3.   Prayer.
4.   Genesis 32.
5.   Heel.

God's command to lead his people to freedom. Each spring, Jews throughout the world retell these Exodus narratives of persecution, liberation, and redemption in their Passover *seder*[6] celebrations.

As the Exodus story unfolds, Moses and the people of Israel face challenge after challenge on their journey from Egypt to the Promised Land. After releasing his slaves from Egyptian servitude, Pharaoh had a change of heart and pursued them to the shore of the Sea of Reeds. Unsure of what to do, Moses prayed to God for deliverance, only to be told to lift up his staff and witness the divine miracle of the parting of the waters. The people passed through unharmed, while the mighty army of Pharaoh drowned in the raging waters after their former slaves' hasty crossing.

The Israelites journeyed to the foot of Mt. Sinai and awaited Moses's meeting with God on the holy mountain. The prophet descended and proclaimed the word of the Lord, only to be shocked and angered by the image of his followers dancing around a golden calf at the foot of the mountain. Moses shattered the stone tablets and was forced to ascend Mt. Sinai again to receive a new set of tablets after he pleaded with God not to destroy this sinful people.

Jewish commentators throughout the ages have discussed and debated the nature of this awesome revelation at Mt. Sinai. Was it the famed Ten Commandments? Perhaps it was the entire Torah—the books of Genesis, Exodus, Leviticus, Numbers, and Deuteronomy. Or the entire Hebrew Bible, known as the Old Testament in Christian tradition. Or, as many traditional Jews posit, Moses received not only the entire Written Law (Torah) but the Oral Law (including later rabbinic works such as the *Mishnah*[7] and *Talmud*[8]) as well. Perhaps Moses was not an ancient scribe who faithfully recorded each and every divine word but a prophet and teacher who communicated with God. In this account of the revelation, the story of the conversations between a gifted human (or humans) and the Holy One became sacred Jewish scripture. Each of these views has its fair share of proponents among Jewish believers and practitioners. What they hold in common is an affirmation that the stories of the Exodus from Egypt and the revelation

---

6. Literally "order," a ritual service and dinner for the first night or two nights of Passover.
7. The first code of Jewish law after the Torah.
8. A compilation of the Mishnah and Gemara, rabbinic discussions of the Mishnah.

at Sinai became the two central motifs of subsequent Jewish thought and practice.

Moses was denied entrance into the Promised Land, and so it was left to his successor, Joshua, to lead the people into the Land of Israel. He, in turn, was succeeded by judges who gathered the Israelite tribes into loose alliances to counter external threats. The judges gave way to prophets, among them Samuel, who agreed to the people's urgent plea to anoint a king to lead them like other nations. Three monarchs—Saul, David, and Solomon—reigned over a united Kingdom of Israel. David captured Jerusalem and made the city the capital of his empire; his son Solomon extended the borders of Israel and built the First Temple in Jerusalem.

The united empire lasted only one hundred years and split apart upon Solomon's death in the tenth century BCE.[9] A revolt led by Jeroboam broke out and led to the formation of two separate kingdoms—Israel in the north comprising ten Israelite tribes headed by Jeroboam, and Judah in the south comprising the tribes of Judah and Benjamin led by Solomon's son Rehoboam. The Hebrew word for Judah (*Yehudah*) becomes the root of the word *yehudim* (Jews) who trace their ancestry to this ancient tribe and most prominent population of the southern kingdom.

Monarchs rose and fell in the north and south, with righteous kings and wicked kings ruling over diminished and weakened nations. They proved to be no match for the rising empires of the ancient Near East. Assyria conquered Israel in 722 BCE and exiled its inhabitants, giving rise to considerable speculation about the ten lost tribes and their ultimate fate. Babylonia conquered Judah in 586 BCE, laid waste to Jerusalem, and destroyed the First Temple. The Babylonian empire gave way to the Persian empire, whose ruler, Cyrus, permitted the exiled Judeans to return to their homeland and rebuild their temple. The Second Temple was dedicated in 515 BCE, later rebuilt and expanded by the Roman procurator Herod and destroyed by the army of the Roman Empire in 70 CE.[10] A section of the outer retaining wall of the Herodian Temple is all that remains today, the holy site revered by Jews as the *Kotel*, the Western Wall (Wailing Wall).

Most ancient peoples abandoned their faith and religious rituals when enemy forces destroyed their central sanctuaries.[11] If their gods failed to

---

9. Before the Common Era; Jewish terminology for BC.
10. Common Era, Jewish terminology for AD.
11. Holy places.

protect their sacred shrines, it was clear that their deities were weaker than those of their enemy and it was time to worship their gods. Not so with the Judeans (Jews) of the ancient Near East. New and unprecedented forms of worship and religious hierarchy emerged out of the ashes of the Second Temple (the central Jewish sanctuary in Jerusalem, destroyed by the Romans in 70 CE). Melakhim[12] and kohanim[13] were stripped of their respective political and religious functions passed down from father to son. Rabbanim[14] assumed leadership roles in Jewish religious life based on scholarship and wisdom rather than lineage. No longer was there a central temple where the people worshiped God through animal sacrifices. Daily prayers and intensive study of scriptural texts became the norms of Jewish religious life. Synagogues, which began to develop after the destruction of the First Temple, became the locus of Jewish communal life, serving as centers of prayer, learning, and assembly. The Jewish people settled into centuries of life in Diaspora[15] communities, though they yearned for a return to their homeland, the Land of Israel.

The rabbinic sages who assumed authority beginning in the first century CE produced the earliest works of postbiblical Jewish law and lore. The *Mishnah* (circa 200 CE) and Babylonian *Talmud* (circa 600 CE) are the literary foundations of Jewish religious life and all subsequent works of *halakhah*.[16] It is important to note that while Jews today trace their origins to Israelite religion and the Hebrew Bible, they are the heirs of rabbinic Judaism that was nurtured and developed in a postbiblical world. Jewish culture, communal life, and thought in the modern world bear little resemblance to their backgrounds in ancient Israel.

A famous text in *Pirkei Avot*[17] recounts the faithful transmission of Torah learning revealed by God to Moses at Sinai, who passed it on to Joshua, then to the elders, next to the prophets, and eventually to rabbinic sages and sets of rabbinic debate partners. The unbroken chain of *shalshelet ha-kabbalah*[18] began with Moses (traditionally referred to as Moshe Rabbenu, "Moses our

---

12. Kings.
13. Priests.
14. Rabbis.
15. Jewish life outside the Land of Israel.
16. Jewish law.
17. Teachings of the Sages, a book in the Mishnah.
18. Jewish tradition.

Rabbi/Teacher") and continued through the Middle Ages with celebrated sages such as the French rabbi and textual commentator Solomon son of Isaac (known by the acronym Rashi) and the Spanish-born rabbi and philosopher Moses Maimonides (known by the acronym Rambam). It continues to this very day when rabbis and other instructors teach sacred texts—Torah, *Mishnah*, *Talmud*, and many others—to their students. This timeless devotion to Jewish learning, known as *talmud Torah*, is the centerpiece of a wide variety of Orthodox and non-Orthodox Jewish educational settings, including *yeshivot*,[19] seminaries for the training of rabbis, *cantors*,[20] teachers, community day schools that provide Jewish and secular instruction, Jewish supplemental schools (often known as religious schools, Hebrew schools, and Sunday schools), seminars, retreats, camps, and others.

Jewish tradition encourages intensive examination and discussion as hallmarks of Jewish learning. Paired learning, known as the *hevrutah* method, is a time-honored educational approach in which two study partners read, analyze, and debate the multiple levels of meaning in a given Jewish text. The rabbinic sage *Hananiah ben Tradyon* taught, "When two persons meet and exchange words of Torah, the *Shekhinah*[21] hovers over them."[22]

Being fully Jewish requires a devotion to lifelong learning. And that learning includes asking questions. Judaism is a faith tradition that welcomes, encourages, and commands its followers to ask questions. Isador Rabi, a Jewish recipient of the Nobel Prize in physics, was once asked why he became a scientist. He explained that his friends and classmates in school returned home each day and were asked, "What did you learn today?" Rabi's mother used to say, "Izzy, did you ask a good question today?" Jewish teachers and Jewish learners ask good questions. This love of learning and questioning is the cornerstone of Jewish religious life and education throughout the ages.

---

19. Traditional rabbinical schools and day schools.
20. Trained members of the clergy who lead music and prayers in synagogues.
21. The Divine Presence.
22. *Pirkei Avot* 3:3.

2

Jewish Beliefs and Doctrines

By Rabbi Mark S. Diamond

Introduction

Judaism is an intricate mixture of theology, religious beliefs, laws, customs, and rituals. Underlying the familiar saying "two Jews, three opinions" is the reality that diversity has been the hallmark of Jewish life since biblical times. There are a seemingly endless variety of individual and communal Jewish expressions in the United States, Israel, and across the globe.

What this means in practical terms is that Latter-day Saints will likely encounter a wide range of theological[1] and practical differences among their Jewish neighbors. Some follow Jewish law strictly and faithfully by carefully observing the Sabbath and holy days, following Jewish dietary restrictions, praying and studying classical Jewish texts each day, and maintaining rules of modesty, gender-based roles, ethical conduct, and additional laws that govern daily living. Other Jews observe Jewish law in modified formats that reflect societal changes such as egalitarian roles for men and women, LGBTQ inclusion, and other contemporary norms. Others shed Jewish practices that they believe have lost relevance in the modern world but retain customs and

---

1. Something based on God's revelation to human beings.

rituals that remain meaningful on a personal or communal level. Still others shun overtly religious expressions of their Jewish identity but proudly call themselves Jews and carry on cultural and ethnic traditions of their heritage.

Conservative, Hasidic, Orthodox, Reconstructionist, Reform, secular, *haredi* (ultra-Orthodox), and "just Jewish" are only a few of the labels Latter-day Saints may hear their Jewish neighbors use to describe their beliefs and practices. This diversity may be unfamiliar and bewildering, but it is the complex reality of Jewish life in the world today. In the sections that follow, we will survey Jewish beliefs, doctrines, customs, and rituals as they are affirmed and practiced by traditionalists, including Hasidic, Orthodox, ultra-Orthodox, and other observant Jews. When appropriate, we will note differences in beliefs and practices among other major sections of the Jewish community. Our primary goal is to expose the layers of Jewish religious life and explore the dynamic and often opposing influences of theological discourse, religious authority, and ethnic and cultural identities among your Jewish neighbors.

God

Monotheism, belief in one and only one God, is the foundational principle of Jewish religious thought. This concept is further developed and refined by the phrase "ethical monotheism," the premise that one God is the ultimate source of human ethics and morality. For Jews, faith in God brings with it the expectation of righteous living to reflect the divine will. To love God is to love and respect God's creations, of which humanity is the highest form on earth.

God is the Eternal One who, by the divine word, created the world—the heavens and the earth, the waters of the seas, the sun, moon, stars, and all creatures and plant life on the planet. The God of Jewish tradition is omniscient and omnipotent—all knowing and all-powerful. God is incorporeal, without body or form of any kind. One of the great challenges in Jewish literary tradition is how to depict an invisible, incorporeal God. Human language and imagery are the only tools we have to describe a God who is truly beyond human description. When we read the Hebrew Bible and rabbinic literature, we find phrases such as the "hand of God" and the "face of God" that describe the Holy One in human terms. God is alternately depicted as a demanding king, a loving father, a fierce warrior, a faithful shepherd, and much more. In a beloved prayer of the Jewish high holy days (Rosh

Hashanah and Yom Kippur), Jews refer to God as *Avinu Malkaynu*[2] as they pray to the Eternal One to move from the throne of justice to the throne of compassion and seal them in the Book of Life for the New Year.

No single image is sufficient to represent God; no single adjective or string of adjectives is adequate to reflect the true essence of God. When Jews are taught that humans are created in God's image, they take this to mean that human conduct should mimic divine conduct. A bold rabbinic text[3] mandates that we provide clothing for the needy just as God clothes the naked;[4] we visit the sick just as God visits the sick;[5] we console mourners just as God consoles mourners;[6] we bury the dead just as God buries the dead.[7] The heart of ethical monotheism is *imitatio dei*—we reflect the image of the one God when we display justice, kindness, and compassion to our fellow human beings.

The very name of the Jewish people—Israel—bears the connotation of one who wrestles with God and struggles with similes and metaphors of the Holy One. Moses Maimonides understood human characteristics used to describe God in the Bible as allegories rather than literal views of the divine. Medieval Jewish mystics described God as the *Ein Sof,* the mysterious "One Without End" who humans can only experience through ten divine emanations, or *sefirot.*[8] In the aftermath of the eighteenth and nineteenth-century Jewish Enlightenment, some Jews began to question traditional views of a supernatural God who works miracles and intervenes directly in human affairs. Leading proponents of existentialist, Reform, Conservative, and Reconstructionist trends in modern Jewish life offer diverse interpretations of God. German philosopher Hermann Cohen viewed God as the set of ideal ethical laws that make up Judaism, what he considered the pure religion of reason. Abraham Joshua Heschel lived in "radical amazement" of God, who is the basis of any being. Mordecai M. Kaplan and other thinkers promote Judaism without supernaturalism and instead view God as "the power that makes for salvation." Still others understand God as limited in

---

2. Our Father, our King.
3. Talmud Tractate Sotah 14a.
4. See Genesis 3:21.
5. See Genesis 18:1.
6. See Genesis 25:11.
7. See Deuteronomy 34:6.
8. Heavenly powers.

power as they confront the horrors of the Holocaust and other manifestations of evil (compare the writings of Richard Rubenstein and Harold Kushner). As with most matters of Jewish thought, we do well to speak of multiple Jewish views of God rather than one single Jewish perspective on the nature of God.

Covenant (*Berit*)

One of the foundational concepts of the Hebrew Bible is the idea of *berit*, covenant. When Noah emerged from his fabled ark, God promised that He would never again destroy creation with a catastrophic flood.[9] Abraham entered into covenants with God on several occasions, notably when the patriarch sought divine reassurance that his new faith would be sustained by future generations. The Mosaic (Moses) and Davidic (King David) covenants extend the divine promise to Abraham that the people of Israel will enjoy a unique relationship with God and a special connection with the Land of Israel.

Scholars note that the character of these ancient covenants differs markedly from one another. Both Noah and Abraham received one-sided divine promises in their encounters with God. In later biblical covenants, there is an explicit two-sided agreement between the two parties. God pledges to bring the people of Israel to the Promised Land and protect and preserve them there if they obey the divine commandments. Simply understood, these later covenants were contracts that specified the rewards for loyalty to God and the penalties for disobedience to the divine will.

When viewed through the lens of a sacred relationship between God and His people, Jewish history may be understood as a cycle of covenants made, covenants broken, and covenants restored. God brought the people of Israel into the Promised Land, only to drive them out at the hands of the Assyrians and Babylonians when they broke their covenant with the Holy One. God restored the people of Judea to their land under benevolent Persian rule, but they were driven out once again by the Romans. Traditionalists explained that Jewish life outside the Land of Israel was *galut*,[10] divine punishment for their sins. The subsequent history of expulsions of Jewish communities from their adopted lands continued for some two thousand years. In a

---

9. Genesis 9.
10. Exile.

familiar refrain, Jewish theologians taught that these communal trials and tribulations were divine chastisements of love, meant to test the faith of the Jewish people and their covenant with God. In traditional Jewish circles, many view the creation of the State of Israel in 1948 as a miracle, a long-awaited restoration of the divine promise to restore the Jews to their ancient homeland.

While Jews today rejoice in Israel and her achievements, many reject the notion of life outside the Land of Israel as divinely ordained exile. They find comfort in traditional Jewish conceptions of *or la-goyim*, the mandate of the Jewish people to serve as a light unto the nations. It was not God's punishment to expel the people from their ancient homeland, they argue. Rather, it was the divine will to send Jews to the four corners of the earth, there to serve as ambassadors of ethical monotheism. This concept is especially prominent in liberal Jewish thought and propels Jews to undertake programs of social justice and social action to bring comfort and healing to a broken world. Jews commonly refer to this as *tikkun olam*.[11]

Messiah (*Mashiah*)

The Hebrew word *mashiah*[12] refers to one who has been anointed for a special calling among the people of Israel. In the Bible, *kohanim*[13] were anointed with holy oil as they took on the rituals and responsibilities of the priesthood; prophets and kings of Israel were anointed with oil to mark the transition to their respective roles as divine spokesmen and monarchs. Later, the term *mashiah* came to be associated with a single unique individual who will be a descendant of King David and serve as monarch of God's holy kingdom on earth. He will be fully human, not a special son of God, since Jewish theology views all human beings as children of God. However, he will possess unique religious and political attributes that God will bestow upon the Messiah and thus enable Him to usher in an era of peace, prosperity, and goodwill for all humankind. This age is known as the Messianic age, and the figure of the Messiah in Jewish thought is fundamentally bound up with the Messianic age. The anointed one who will usher in the Messianic

---

11. Literally "repair of the world."
12. Literally "anointed."
13. Priests.

age is the Messiah; anyone who fails to do so is not the Messiah in the eyes of Jewish tradition.

It is not surprising that Jewish thinkers have different views of the qualities of the long-awaited Messiah and precisely what will happen in the Messianic age. Some Jews look forward to a time marked by the reunification of the ancient tribes of Israel, the return of Jews across the globe to the Land of Israel, the restoration of all Jews to full observance of Jewish law, the rebuilding of the great Temple in Jerusalem, and ultimately the reign of universal peace. The prophet Isaiah envisioned a miraculous era during which the laws of nature would be disrupted, a time when rival species in the animal kingdom will no longer prey on one another. Others foretold catastrophic disruptions and wars of Gog and Magog as preludes to the Messianic era. Still others contended that the Messianic age would not be a time of great miracles. Moses Maimonides elaborated on this view of Messianic times:

> Do not presume that in the Messianic age any facet of the world's nature will change or there will be innovations in the work of creation. Rather, the world will continue according to its pattern. Although Isaiah 11:6 states: "The wolf will dwell with the lamb, the leopard will lie down with the young goat," these words are a metaphor and a parable. . . . Our sages taught: "There will be no difference between the current age and the Messianic era except the emancipation of our subjugation to the kingdoms of the world."[14]

Although he did not endorse all of the prophetic images of Messianic times, Maimonides steadfastly affirmed belief in a Messiah as one of his Thirteen Principles of Faith: "I believe with perfect faith in the coming of the Messiah, and even though he may tarry, I await him on the day that he will come." This famous passage, adapted from Maimonides's writings and later set to music, was the haunting refrain sung by many Jews as they walked to the gas chambers of Nazi death camps. In the dark nights of the Holocaust, and in other historical periods of severe antisemitic (anti-Jewish) persecution, Jews found comfort in the vision of a time when God's Messiah would come to erase the pain of human suffering on earth.

---

14. Maimonides, *Mishneh Torah*, Laws of Kings and Wars, 12:1–2.

A longstanding debate among Jewish thinkers centers on the respective roles of God and human beings in bringing about the Messianic era. Are we to wait patiently for the Messiah's arrival at the divinely appointed time, or do we have a role to play in creating a world that is ready for the Messiah and shares some of the characteristics of the Messianic era? Some Jews and non-Jews throughout history have predicted the precise date of the Messiah's arrival or proclaimed that a particular individual was the long-awaited Messiah. Most rabbis strongly discouraged these practices and refuted the Messianic claims of a series of false Messiahs, notably the Jewish military leader Simeon Bar Kokhba in the second century and the charismatic mystic Sabbetai Zevi in the seventeenth century. The ancient sage Rabbi Johanan ben Zakkai taught that if a person is planting a tree when others announce that the Messiah has come, finish planting the tree and then go out to greet him. In a poignant Talmudic fable, Rabbi Joshua ben Levi met the Messiah and asked when He will come. The latter replied, "Today." Later, Rabbi Joshua met the prophet Elijah, the herald of the Messiah according to Jewish tradition. The rabbi complained, "The Messiah lied to me, since he told me he was coming today but he did not do so." Elijah responded: "He told you that he will come 'today, if you will but hearken to his voice.'"[15] God will send the Messiah one day, but we must do our share to prepare for that day and be ready and willing to recognize the Messiah when He does arrive.

Although belief in a divinely ordained Messiah is a traditional Jewish doctrine, many Jews today reject the notion that one special individual will be sent by God to redeem the world. There is a widely shared belief among non-Orthodox Jews that human action and human action alone will usher in an era of peace and goodwill on earth. They hold that deeds of love and kindness—feeding the hungry, clothing the naked, housing the homeless, reducing weapons of war, advocating for peace—are direct actions we must undertake to move the world closer to time-honored visions of Messianic times. Editors of numerous prayer books of the non-Orthodox Jewish movements have removed traditional references to the figure of the Messiah and substituted language that refers to a utopian era of universal peace and prosperity.

Latter-day Saints may encounter individuals who call themselves Messianic Jews, Hebrew Christians, or Jews for Jesus. These are men and

---

15. Psalm 95:7.

women who proclaim their Jewish identity but also believe in Jesus as the Messiah.[16] Often they observe traditional Jewish practices such as *Shabbat*[17] and kashrut,[18] and they pray in congregations that substitute the Hebrew name *Yeshua* for *Jesus*. Many of these congregations and their parent bodies are funded and supported by evangelical Christian organizations that single out Jews as the objects of special missionary campaigns.

Latter-day Saints should recognize and appreciate the highly critical standard Jewish response to these groups. As noted above, the Jewish view of the Messiah cannot be severed from the Jewish view of the Messianic age. While Jews respect their Christian friends and neighbors as fellow monotheists who believe in Jesus as the Messiah and the Son of God, they understand that belief as the fundamental difference between Christianity and Judaism. Jews of most every stream of Jewish life and thought—Orthodox and non-Orthodox, religious and secular—share the view that a Jew who believes in Jesus Christ has passed through a theological boundary and removed himself or herself from the Jewish community as it defines itself. This deep-seated view is rooted not only in Jewish theology but also in Jewish history filled with antisemitic violence and forced conversions (falsely) done in the name of the Prince of Peace. Jews cherish the fundamental principles of religious liberty that allow people to freely express their own religious beliefs and practices. However, they are troubled by groups they view as spiritual fraudulent, and they take great offense at campaigns that claim that one can only be a "good Jew" or a "fulfilled Jew" by becoming a Jew for Jesus or a Messianic Jew. Latter-day Saints do well to appreciate the challenging fact that their Jewish neighbors may have difficulty articulating what they believe in, but they know quite well what they *don't* believe in.

This World and the World to Come (*Olam Haba*)

Jewish beliefs and practices are grounded in a "this worldly" view of existence, namely that our lives on earth are of limited span and we are expected to lead lives of purpose and meaning. The Torah introduces the foundational concept of *kedushah*.[19] Holy words and holy deeds reflect the divine

---

16. *Mashiah*, or Christ; the Greek translation of the Hebrew *Mashiah*.
17. The Sabbath.
18. The Jewish dietary laws.
19. Holiness or sanctity.

image within us and bring us closer to God, family, and community. Jewish law provides a detailed list of 613 *mitzvot*[20] that imbue our lives with holiness by performing certain actions (positive commandments) and refraining from others (negative commandments). When a Jew begins a blessing with the traditional language—"Praised are You, Lord our God, Sovereign of the Universe, who has commanded us"—he or she is transforming an ordinary act into a sacred rite. Blessings over food and drink, daily prayers, special blessings to usher in sacred days on the calendar, and blessings to mark life-cycle milestones all serve to foster a spirit of holiness in our lives.

In Jewish tradition, an act that brings honor to God is called *kiddush haShem*, a deed that sanctifies God's sacred name. Ethical conduct is the hallmark of a Jew who strives to live by the principles of his or her faith. Conversely, one whose behavior is unethical is guilty of *hillul HaShem*, a deed that dishonors God, family, and community. Most every faith community has members who faithfully follow the detailed rules and regulations of prayer and ritual observance, only to act unethically toward their fellow men and women. So too among Jews, some of whom profess to love God and meticulously observe God's laws but mistreat others in word or deed. These behavioral lapses point to a disconnect between their ritual conduct on the one hand and their ethical conduct on the other. Truly, we honor God when we follow God's laws *and* demonstrate love and compassion for our fellow human beings.

For many Jews, righteous living in this world is a reward in and of itself. Others look to traditional Jewish texts that promise perpetual reward in *olam haba*.[21] Jewish views of eternal life are many and varied. Some rabbinic works describe the world to come as a heavenly paradise, a reward for righteous living on earth. Others depict what happens when a person dies and the soul departs from the body. These texts promise a reunification of body and soul when the Messiah comes to redeem the world. This rabbinic concept is called *tehiyat ha-maytim*.[22] Thrice daily, observant Jews recite a prayer that praises God for the miracle of resurrecting the dead in the end of days and making bodies and souls whole again as they were on earth.

Not all religious Jews affirm the traditional view of bodily resurrection and reunification of body and soul. Classical prayer books of the Conservative

---

20. Literally "commandments."
21. The world to come.
22. Literally "resurrection of the dead."

Jewish movement retained the traditional Hebrew text but translated the prayer to read, "Praised are You, Lord our God, who calls the dead to life everlasting." Classical Reform prayer books altered the Hebrew language of this supplication and translated it as, "Praised are You, Lord our God, who gives life to all." Recently revised prayer books in the Reform Jewish movement offer both options in the Hebrew text and creative English translations as well. These developments reflect the discomfort of many modern Jews to affirm beliefs that run counter to the worldviews that became current in nineteenth-century rationalism.

The Jewish People and Peoplehood

A primary feature of the traditional Jewish view of *berit* (covenant) is the idea that Jews are *am segulah*.[23] In the words of the Torah, "For you are a people consecrated to the Lord your God; the Lord your God chose you from among all other peoples on earth to be His treasured people."[24] One God, the God of the entire universe, selected one people, the people of Israel, to live in one land, the Promised Land of Israel. This covenant bound God's people to faithfully follow the laws found in the Torah, the divine revelation received by Moses and the people of Israel at Mt. Sinai that is lovingly passed on from generation to generation.

It is commonplace for faith communities to believe that they and they alone have a unique relationship with God. After all, why should a person support a set of religious beliefs and follow a code of religious practices if they are not based on a special connection with God, a relationship not enjoyed by those who think and act differently? This view of religious truth, known as religious exclusivism (there can be only one truth), is a feature of classical monotheistic (based on belief in one God alone) religious thought. Yet it raises profound questions of how to understand the divine plan for a world marked by diverse religious, ethnic, racial, and national identities. Traditional Jewish thinkers respond to this challenge by noting that Judaism is the true path for Jews, not necessarily for all of humanity. God expects His chosen people to follow the 613 *mitzvot* of their special Jewish legacy; God has different standards for other peoples and doesn't necessarily expect

---

23. The chosen or treasured people of God.
24. Deuteronomy 14:2.

them to embrace the Jewish faith. As the first-century sage Rabbi Joshua taught, "The righteous of all peoples have a share in the world to come."[25]

Some modern Jewish thinkers reinterpret or reject the Chosen People doctrine as being inherently undemocratic and even racist. If God selected the Jewish people as His unique treasure, they argue, this implies that others are "unchosen." Mordecai M. Kaplan rejected the doctrine of the Jewish people as God's uniquely chosen people. He even revised prayers in the *siddur*[26] to remove any references to this doctrine. Instead, Kaplan posited that all peoples have their own mission or mandate, and Jews likewise have a special purpose to fulfill as the heirs of an ancient, evolving religious civilization.

Both for Jews who affirm that the Jewish people are God's treasured people and for those who reinterpret or deny this principle, there is general agreement that peoplehood is arguably the most critical feature of Jewish life and thought. Judaism is an ethnic category, but individuals who formally convert to Judaism ("Jews by Choice") are fully Jewish and are recognized as such by Jewish tradition and the Jewish community. Judaism is most assuredly a religion, but Jews who are "not religious" consider themselves Jewish and are accepted as such by their fellow Jews.

This may well be confusing and even troubling for Latter-day Saints for whom faith defines their religious identity and is the decisive factor that makes them Latter-day Saints. This isn't so with Jews, since Jewish identity may be rooted in lineage, religion, culture, ethnicity, community, nationality, or a combination of these characteristics. Jews who pray three times daily and observe the dietary laws and Sabbath regulations are Jewish. Jews who attend synagogue services twice a year on the holy days of *Rosh Hashanah* and *Yom Kippur* are Jewish, as are those who light *Hanukkah* candles and hold a Passover *seder* at home but do not observe other Jewish holidays in public or private. So too are Jews who are atheistic or agnostic and eat traditional Jewish foods each week and count themselves as Jewish by virtue of a parent's Jewish status. As are Jews who are not religious but are vocal defenders of the State of Israel and Jewish communities in the Diaspora.

If there is one element that unites Jews around the globe, it is identification with the Jewish people past, present, and future. A Jew living in

---

25. *Tosefta* Sanhedrin 13:3.
26. Jewish prayer book.

Salt Lake City likely feels a special bond with a Jew living in New York, Jerusalem, St. Petersburg, or Paris. Religious or not, Jews tend to take seriously the Talmudic dictum, *kol Yisrael arayvim zeh la-zeh*: "All Jews are responsible for one another." In times of crisis, Jewish communities muster their financial and human resources to rescue endangered Jews and combat antisemitism[27] at home and abroad. When Jews in the former Soviet Union were persecuted and even imprisoned for declaring their intent to leave their motherland and live as proud, free people in Israel, their fellow Jews in the United States staged public rallies and lobbied officials in Washington, DC and the Kremlin to "free Soviet Jews." When a synagogue was attacked in Pittsburgh and a terrorist bomb exploded in Tel Aviv, Jews shared the pain of the victims and demonstrated solidarity and sympathy with their fellow Jews thousands of miles away. In an age of heightened prejudice and a sharp increase in acts of hatred and violence toward minorities, Jews are especially sensitive to the alarming escalation of antisemitic rhetoric and violence in many parts of the globe. Over the course of three millennia, Jewish communities have been founded and sustained on the pillars of self-protection, communal responsibility, and self-reliance.

The Talmudic statement that Jews are responsible for one another is more than a rallying cry in times of communal crisis and peril. It led to the establishment of a plethora of Jewish organizations and institutions to care for Jews "from cradle to grave." Throughout history, Jewish leaders have assumed the obligation of providing educational and social welfare services for their communities. Scholars date the roots of universal Jewish education to the second century of the Common Era, when the Sanhedrin[28] "president" Simeon ben Shetah ordered schools to be established across Judea to educate children in Torah and Jewish law. Later, Jews developed networks of educational centers—nursery schools, elementary and secondary schools, Jewish seminaries and universities, supplemental and adult education programs, Jewish camps, retreats, and other informal educational opportunities—to realize the Jewish vision of lifelong learning for all.

Centuries ago, Jewish orphanages were formed to care for young children without a parent; Jewish family service agencies offered and continue to offer counseling services; Jewish vocational service agencies provide job

---

27. Hostility toward Jewish people.
28. The Jewish Supreme Court in ancient Jerusalem.

training and vocational guidance; Jewish-run soup kitchens feed the hungry; Jewish groups manage the wedding details and expenses of needy Jewish brides; Jewish centers for senior adults provide dignified living options and health care for older Jews; Jewish burial societies comfort mourners and take care of funeral and burial arrangements; Jewish hospitals care for the special needs of Jewish patients and offered internships and residencies to Jewish physicians in an era when they could not obtain similar opportunities at medical centers sponsored by other religious communities.

Today, some of these organizations and institutions no longer exist because the Jewish community's needs and priorities have changed. Many others have expanded their roles to serve gentiles as well as Jews. Jewish hospitals and medical centers welcome patients and staff members of all faiths or no faith. Jewish family services, vocational services, and clothing and food distribution projects serve mostly non-Jewish clients in cities across the United States. In so doing, they fulfill yet another Jewish precept rooted in the words of the prophet Jeremiah: "Seek the welfare of the city to which I have exiled you and pray to the Lord on its behalf; for in its welfare you shall find your welfare."[29]

The financial foundation of Jewish educational and social welfare endeavors is *tzedakah*. While *tzedakah* is most often translated as "charity," the term is more properly understood as "righteous giving," from the Hebrew root that means "justice" or "righteousness." Charity derives from the Latin word *caritas*, meaning "generous love," and implies that love is the basis of helping others. By contrast, *tzedakah* is not predicated on love; the *mitzvah*[30] to help others is a sacred Jewish obligation. Jews are duty bound to give *tzedakah* generously whether or not they feel love for the recipient or even know the recipient. Indeed, Maimonides stated that one of the highest types of *tzedakah* is anonymous giving in which neither the donor nor the recipient knows the identity of the other. Curiously, the highest type of giving according to Maimonides is to support someone with a gift or loan, or by setting up a partnership, or by finding employment for the person in need so that he or she will not be dependent on the community. Sustaining others before they become impoverished is a higher priority than the preference for anonymity in acts of *tzedakah*.

---

29. Jeremiah 2:7.
30. Commandment.

In self-governing communities prior to the Emancipation,[31] Jews were taxed by their own authorities to fund communal needs. Today, Jews provide generous amounts of *tzedakah* voluntarily to a wide variety of worthy causes—synagogues, schools, social service agencies, advocacy organizations, and many more. In addition, they contribute generously to many other philanthropic causes—universities, museums, medical centers, cultural and artistic endeavors, and so on. Jewish philanthropists and organizational leaders engage in passionate discussion and debate about how to distribute their *tzedakah* contributions—how much to donate to specifically Jewish causes versus broader civic causes, and how much to donate to projects in Israel versus projects in the Jewish Diaspora. It is difficult to reach consensus on these emotional issues, save for agreement that there are never enough funds to meet all the critical needs in local communities, in Israel, and across the nation and the world.

Jewish Tribes, Sects, and Movements

The age-old question of what makes one Jewish presents fundamental challenges for scholars and communal leaders, as well as "regular Jews." While patriarchal descent seems to have defined Israelite identity in the Bible, matriarchal descent became the norm in Jewish life in the rabbinic period. One whose mother is Jewish or formally embraces the Jewish faith through conversion is considered a Jew. As noted above, there are religious Jews, secular Jews, Jews with labels, Jews without labels ("just Jewish"), and a host of other identifications.

In the biblical period, the Israelites were divided into twelve tribal designations named for the sons and grandsons of the patriarch Jacob. The northern kingdom of Israel was made up of ten tribes—Reuben, Simeon, Manasseh, Issachar, Zebulon, Ephraim, Dan, Gad, Asher, and Naphtali—while the southern kingdom of Judea comprised two tribes, Judah and Benjamin. According to the biblical account, each tribe received an allotment of territory in the Land of Israel. Descendants of Levi, one of the sons of Jacob, did not receive any land. Instead, they were singled out for a special purpose: to act as assistants to the *kohanim*,[32] the descendants of Aaron

---

31. The process of eliminating restrictions on European Jews and granting them citizenship rights in the late eighteenth and nineteenth centuries.
32. Priests.

who served God in the sacred rituals of the tabernacle and temple worship. *Kohanim* were supported and sustained by the other tribes of Israel through an elaborate system of tithing.

Tribal distinctions no longer serve a function in contemporary Jewish life, save for the threefold designation of *kohen*,[33] *levi*,[34] and *yisrael*.[35] *Kohanim*, modern-day Jews who claim descent from the ancient priests, receive and bestow special honors in traditional synagogues. They are called upon to bless the other worshipers on festivals and are granted the first honor of blessing the Torah[36] during public readings of scripture on Monday and Thursday mornings and during Sabbath and festival services. *Levi'im*, Levites who claim descent from the tribe of Levi, receive the second Torah honor on such occasions and wash the hands of *kohanim* prior to their blessing the congregation. In Reform, Reconstructionist, and many Conservative synagogues, there is no distinction between the three categories of Jews; *kohanim* and *levi'im* do not receive any special roles in religious rituals in these congregations.

In lieu of tribal designations, modern Jews may be categorized by geographic origin and/or Jewish denomination. Three broad classifications distinguish Jews by their geographic roots:

Ashkenazi: The word derives from *Ashkenaz*, the traditional Hebrew name of Germany. *Ashkenazi* (or *Ashkenazic*) Jews trace their ancestry to Jews who began living in Germany between the fifth and thirteenth centuries. From there, Jews migrated throughout Central, Western, and Eastern Europe, Russia, North America, and Israel. At times, *Ashkenazi* Jews flourished and attained great heights of learning, culture, and religious revival. At other times, Jewish communities in Germany, Poland, and Russia suffered terrible persecution, violence, death, and communal destruction at the hands of medieval Crusaders, Cossacks, and frenzied mobs that accused their Jewish neighbors of ritual murder, host desecration,[37] and poisoning the wells of Europe during the Black Death. During the Holocaust, the Nazis

---

33. Priest.
34. Levite.
35. Israelite; now known as "Jew."
36. An honor in which a worshipper reads or chants a special blessing before and after the public recitation of a portion of scripture.
37. A serious sin in Catholicism and Orthodox Christian denominations, here used to describe a bizarre accusation that Jews stole the consecrated bread used in the mass and then tortured the body of Christ.

and their willing accomplices relied on a sordid history of European anti-semitism to murder six million Jews, most of them *Ashkenazim*, throughout Europe.

Sephardi: The word comes from *Sepharad*, the Hebrew term for Spain. *Sephardi* (or *Sephardic*) Jews trace their roots back to the proud and noble Jewish communities of Spain, where they flourished from the eighth to the fifteenth centuries in a period often called the Golden Age of Spanish Jewry. Famed *Sephardi* scholars such as Maimonides (Rabbi Moshe ben Maimon), Nahmanides (Rabbi Moshe ben Nahman, no relation to Maimonides), and Rabbi Moses de Leon wrote classic works of Torah commentary, Jewish law, philosophy, and mystical literature. Jews were expelled from Spain in 1492, the same year that Christopher Columbus sailed to the New World. Both acts—one a black mark on Spain and the Spanish monarchy, the other a celebrated milestone in world history—were undertaken on the orders of King Ferdinand and Queen Isabella.

Following the Spanish expulsion and the horrors of the Spanish and Portuguese Inquisitions, *Sephardi* Jews migrated to the Ottoman Empire (Turkey), the Netherlands, Greece, North Africa, Israel, and North America. *Sephardi* Jews who lived under Muslim rule were considered *dhimmi*, mono-theists who had a status that was inferior to Muslims but higher than many other subjects of their respective countries. Following the establishment of the State of Israel in 1948, anti-Jewish riots erupted in many Middle Eastern countries and forced most *Sephardi* Jews to immigrate to Israel.

Mizrahi: The word is derived from the Hebrew *mizrah*, meaning "east." Jews who come from the so-called Edot Ha-Mizrah[38] are sometimes referred to as Oriental Jews and are descendants of ancient Jewish communities that existed in the Middle East and North Africa since biblical days. They include a variety of Jewish subcommunities—Iraqi, Persian, Syrian, Yemenite, Bukharan, Jews from Kurdistan and Georgia, and the mountain Jews of Azerbaijan and Dagestan. Like *Ashkenazi* and *Sephardi* Jews, *Mizrahi* Jews have their own sets and subsets of religious rites, customs, and foods unique to their countries of origin. Today, most *Mizrahi* Jews live in Israel. There the majority of Jews are *Sephardi*, while *Ashkenazi* Jews form the second largest classification of the Israeli Jewish population. In North America and Europe, most Jews are *Ashkenazim*, with substantial *Sephardi*

---

38. "Communities of the East."

Jewish communities in major American and European cities. Intermarriage between *Ashkenazi, Sephardi,* and *Mizrahi* Jews in Israel and elsewhere has eroded many of the traditional distinctions between these groups and makes it difficult for demographers to accurately identify and define them in the twenty-first century.

Jewish movements and denominations may be said to date from the Second Temple period (515 BCE to 70 CE). During this era in Jewish history, sects multiplied among the Jews as they responded to successive waves of Persian, Hellenistic (Greek), and Roman control of the Land of Israel. Pro-Hellenist and anti-Hellenist forces fought bitter battles for control of Jewish life under Greco-Syrian rule. In Roman times, Pharisees, Sadducees, Essenes, zealots, and other factions offered contrasting views of Jewish autonomy and accommodation to foreign influences. Eventually, all but the Pharisees and their rabbinic heirs disappeared from history.

The multiple varieties of Jewish life and thought today reflect diverse responses to and adaptations of rabbinic Judaism. Hasidic Judaism is a branch of *haredi*[39] Judaism that originated in Eastern Europe in the eighteenth century with the teachings and tales of Rabbi Israel ben Eliezer, known as the Baal Shem Tov.[40] He was a roving preacher, teacher, mystic, and healer who rebelled against the harsh doctrines and practices of the Orthodox Jewish world of his day and age. The *Besht*[41] built upon the mystical beliefs of medieval Lurianic *Kabbalah* (mysticism) and taught his disciples and followers to draw closer to God and redeem the divine holy sparks in everyone and everything around them. He shunned the Talmudic *pilpul*[42] that was common in traditional *yeshivot* and the rabbis' prescription of harsh practices to counteract the dread and gloom of Jewish life in the eighteenth century. The *Besht* attracted masses of Jews to his simple, pious expressions of Jewish worship and ritual life that stressed joyous prayer, song, and dance. For Hasidic sects, then and now, their religious leaders are more than rabbis—they are charismatic *rebbes* with special powers to sway the divine will and fill their followers' lives with ultimate purpose and meaning. The *Besht* and his successors established Hasidic sects led by *rebbes* who typically

---

39. Literally "one who trembles" at the word of God, meaning ultra-Orthodox.
40. Literally "Master of the Good Name."
41. An invented name made up of the first letters of Baal Shem Tov.
42. Intense analysis of texts to resolve apparent contradictions.

inherit the mantle of leadership through dynastic succession—father to son, father to son-in-law, and so on.

Many rabbis and their followers were bitter opponents of the early *Hasidim*, and they became known as *mitnagdim* or *misnagdim*.[43] The two groups waged fierce rhetorical battles for the hearts and minds of Europe's Jews, disputes that sometimes descended into outright violence and bans of herem[44] pronounced upon the opposition. With the passage of time, the split between Hasidim and mitnagdim declined, thanks to a curb on the extremes of Hasidic fervor, a return to traditional Jewish scholarship in Hasidic circles, and intermarriage between the two groups.

Above all, both groups of *haredi* (ultra-Orthodox) Jews largely put aside their differences when they found a common enemy in the *Haskalah*, the Jewish Enlightenment that was attracting large numbers of Jews to new forms and expressions of Jewish identity. Chief among them was Reform Judaism, which first developed in Germany in the nineteenth century and was led by rabbis who sought to harmonize Jewish belief and practices on the one hand and Enlightenment thought on the other. The German Reformers introduced prayers and sermons in the spoken language of the land, mixed seating of men and women, organs, and choirs into Jewish worship services. They eased or eliminated traditional laws of *kashrut*[45] and *Shabbat*[46] observance for newly emancipated Jews who chose to attend universities and embark on new career opportunities. They were met with fierce opposition by three "camps" of Orthodox Jews—*Hasidim* and *mitnagdim*, who condemned secular education and shunned Enlightenment thought, and a new group known as "neo-Orthodox" Jews, who championed the efficacy of both secular and traditional Jewish education and affirmed a new, modern Orthodox Jewish lifestyle in a post-Enlightenment world.

Despite the steadfast opposition of traditionalists, Reform congregations thrived in Germany and throughout Western and Central Europe. With the founding in 1875 of Cincinnati's Hebrew Union College (HUC), the first rabbinical seminary in America, Reform Judaism rapidly took hold in large and small Jewish communities throughout the United States. Today, Reform Judaism is the largest of the Jewish movements or denominations

---

43. Literally "opponents."
44. Excommunication.
45. Jewish dietary restrictions.
46. The Sabbath.

in North America, though it has shed some of its classical principles and embraced a renewal of traditional Jewish practices such as Hebrew prayer and *Shabbat* rituals.

Like its Reform counterpart, Conservative Judaism first developed in Germany as a response to the Enlightenment and flourished once it reached American shores. Early Conservative Jewish leaders felt that the Reformers had gone too far in shedding Jewish traditions, especially the use of Hebrew in prayer services. New York's Jewish Theological Seminary (JTS) was established in 1886 as the educational center of Conservative Judaism and an alternative to the Hebrew Union College and the Orthodox community's Rabbi Isaac Elchanan Theological Seminary, chartered in 1897 and now part of New York's Yeshiva University. When the founders of Conservative Judaism selected a name for their new movement, they intended the word "conservative" to convey their desire to conserve traditional Jewish thought and practice, not a political ideology in opposition to liberal or progressive thinking.

Yet another Jewish movement, Reconstructing Judaism (formerly called Reconstructionism), owes its origin to the writings of Rabbi Mordecai M. Kaplan, a professor at the Jewish Theological Seminary whose magnum opus, *Judaism as a Civilization*, called for a radical rethinking of Jewish communal life and religious thought. Kaplan conceived of Reconstructionist Judaism as a more progressive stream within the Conservative Jewish movement; his disciples broke with Conservative Judaism and launched their own movement in 1955 and their own rabbinical college in Philadelphia in 1967. The contemporary Jewish religious landscape is thus made up of Conservative, Hasidic, Orthodox, Reconstructionist, Reform, and ultra-Orthodox Jews with their respective synagogues and international associations of rabbis, cantors, and congregations (synagogues). There are also Jewish Renewal congregations, humanistic synagogues, and unaffiliated congregations whose members eschew traditional movement and denominational labels.

As noted above, this picture of Jewish religious life can be bewildering and even intimidating for Latter-day Saints who want to understand their Jewish neighbors. As a general guideline to the beliefs and practices of the major Jewish movements, we can say the following: Reform, Reconstructionist, and Renewal congregations are the most progressive in terms of Jewish thought and practice; Conservative congregations are more traditional in conserving Jewish practices but also support equal religious roles for women and men like their progressive counterparts; Orthodox congregations are still more traditional in their loyalty to Jewish law; and ultra-Orthodox and Hasidic congregations are the strictest in their adherence to the norms of *halakhah*.[47] Within a given synagogue, there will likely be a wide variety of customs and rituals observed by congregants, and even greater variety in the Jewish community at large. Moreover, Jews often choose to become members of a particular synagogue based less on ideology and more on other factors, including geographic proximity, the availability of daycare and nursery school programs, educational opportunities for children and adults, and friendships with rabbis, staff members, and congregants of a given synagogue. Jews are free to choose which synagogue, if any, to affiliate with, and they may change congregational membership several times in larger communities with multiple synagogue options. Such is the nature of contemporary Jewish life, a fascinating puzzle with thousands of pieces that comprise the whole.

Israel—The Land and the State

Jews have a special bond with *eretz Yisrael*[48] dating back to the patriarchs and matriarchs of Jewish tradition and the origins of the tribes of Israel. With the conquest of the northern tribes of Israel in 722 BCE and the southern tribes of Judea in 586 BCE and again in 70 CE, Jewish independence ceased, and the focus of Jewish life shifted from the Land of Israel to the lands of the Diaspora. Yet the Jewish heart and soul continued to yearn for a return to Israel. Daily prayers call upon God to "return in mercy to Jerusalem Your city"; the concluding refrain of the *Yom Kippur* service in synagogues and the Passover *seder* in Jewish homes proclaims the hope that those who celebrate will be able to come together "next year in Jerusalem." Synagogues throughout the world place the Holy Ark (an enclosure that houses the sacred Torah scrolls) on the wall facing Jerusalem to orient worshipers to face the holy city in prayer. Jews in the West often place a small piece of artwork known as a *mizrah*[49] in their homes to direct their thoughts toward the Land of Israel. These are all manifestations of the centrality of Israel and Jerusalem in Jewish thought and practice. They give tangible expression to the poetic longing of the Psalmist: "If I forget you,

---

47. The corpus of Jewish law.
48. The Land of Israel.
49. Literally "east."

O Jerusalem, let my right hand wither; let my tongue stick to my palate if I cease to think of you, if I do not keep Jerusalem in memory even at my happiest hour."[50]

Even when life in foreign lands seemed safe, secure, and comfortable, Jews longed for a return to their ancient homeland. With the first stirrings of modern political Zionism[51] in the nineteenth century, Jews began to transform their ancient dream into reality. Antisemitism was rife throughout central and Eastern Europe and led to devastating persecution of Jews. Violent pogroms[52] decimated vibrant Jewish communities in Poland, Russia, Ukraine, and elsewhere. Theodor Herzl, a Vienna-based Jewish journalist, argued that the time had come for Jews to leave their adopted lands and settle in the Land of Israel. At first, small groups of Jews embarked on the herculean task of making *aliyah*,[53] a term used to describe immigration to Palestine, as the Land of Israel was known at the time. With the advent of the twentieth century, successive waves of *aliyah* brought tens of thousands of Jews to Palestine. In the aftermath of the Holocaust, and with the founding of the State of Israel in 1948, hundreds of thousands of Jews immigrated to Israel. Today the population of the State of Israel is more than 8.5 million people, of whom 6.7 million are Jewish.

Zionism is a word that is often misunderstood by its proponents and its detractors. Zionism is the national movement for the return of the Jewish people to their homeland and the reestablishment of Jewish independence in the Land of Israel. With the birth of the nation of Israel in 1948, the term *Zionism* now includes the movement for the development and protection of the State of Israel. Perhaps the most enduring legacy of modern Zionism is the remarkable (and many would say miraculous) transformation of *am Yisrael*[54] from a persecuted, stateless, homeless people to a proud, resilient, independent people with an ancient homeland and a powerful nation state of its own.

There is no one single stream of Jewish thought that we can properly call Zionism. Rather, there are multiple strands of Zionist ideology—political,

---

50. Psalm 137:5.
51. The movement to re-establish (and now strengthen and support) the Jewish nation in the Land of Israel.
52. Anti-Jewish riots.
53. Literally "ascent."
54. The Jewish people.

religious, cultural, Labor Zionism, Revisionist Zionism, and Diaspora Zionism. Some of these are connected to Israeli political movements and parties that helped to create the State of Israel and its governmental institutions. Others are the product of Zionist thinkers who had contrasting views of what a Jewish state should embody and embrace—Jewish culture, Jewish religious law, a safe haven for oppressed Jews, socialism, capitalism, and so on. Classical Zionist thinkers and the early leaders of the State of Israel believed that all Jews should make *aliyah*; they were firmly convinced that integration of Jews outside Israel would lead inevitably to the demise of Diaspora Jewish life. Today, most Jews recognize that there are vibrant centers of Jewish life both in Israel and in the Diaspora, and each center needs the other.

A large majority of Jews in the world support a vibrant and secure State of Israel. They contribute generously to Israeli institutions and Diaspora-based organizations that advocate for Israel's security and promote ties between Israel, the United States, and other countries throughout the world. AIPAC (the American Israel Public Affairs Committee) convened 18,000 people in Washington, DC in recent years for its policy conference, formerly the largest annual Jewish gathering in the world. Non-Jews as well as Jews are active participants in AIPAC and many other Israel-centered causes. In recent years, Christian Zionists have assumed a significant role in supporting Israel with their lobbying efforts, financial resources, and pilgrimage tours to the Holy Land.

While most Jews and many non-Jews are deeply committed to Israel, there is a broad diversity of opinion on how best to manifest their Zionist commitment. Just as patriotic Americans are loyal to their country but may disagree with priorities of a given US president and Congress, patriotic Israelis and Diaspora Zionists are loyal to Israel but may criticize policies of a given Israeli prime minister and the *Knesset*.[55] Zionists are keenly aware of the external threats Israel faces from unstable, hostile neighbors in the region, as well as terrorist forces on its borders and within Israel itself. Some Jews and non-Jews are critical of Israeli policies toward Arab Israelis and Palestinians living in the West Bank and Gaza. Among them are individuals and organizations that endorse a two-state solution—a call for a peaceful democratic State of Israel and a peaceful democratic state of Palestine

---

55. Israel's parliament.

to share the Holy Land. Others advocate a one-state solution that would have Israel control the entire land with limited rights and autonomy for Palestinians. Still others propose a binational state with equal rights for Palestinian and Israeli citizens.

There is no lack of opinions within Israel and the Diaspora on contentious questions of security, democratic values, minority rights, the role of religion in a Jewish majority state, Israel–Diaspora relations, and other complex issues facing Israel today. Jews, Latter-day Saints, and all those who yearn for peace in the Middle East, do well to recognize that the internal and external challenges Israel confronts are complicated and do not lend themselves to short sound bites on social media and other news sources. There is no adequate substitute for visiting Israel to tour holy sites and meet holy people—Christians, Druze, Jews, Muslims, and others—living in the Holy Land. And, of course, there is the power of prayer: "Pray for the well-being of Jerusalem; may those who love you be at peace."[56]

On October 7, 2023, Hamas, the terrorist organization that controls Gaza, launched a series of brutal and deadly terrorist attacks in Israel. This shocking assault on the Jewish holy day of Simhat Torah resulted in the murder of some 1,400 Israelis, the kidnapping of more than 200 men, women, and children, and unspeakable acts of sexual violence against women and young girls. The vast majority of the victims of the Hamas attacks were peace-loving, innocent civilians who lived in Israel proper rather than in settlements in the disputed West Bank.

In response to this unprecedented assault, the Israel Defence Forces (IDF) entered Gaza with the goals to dismantle the Hamas infrastructure and free Israeli captives. As of this writing, the ongoing Israel–Hamas War has led to the deaths of more than 200 Israeli soldiers, thousands of Hamas terrorists, and more than 20,000 Gaza residents. The war has brought terrible suffering to innocent people, especially children, both in Israel and Gaza. We mourn the loss of these precious lives.

In a further shock felt around the world, the Hamas attacks sparked new waves of antisemitism and anti-Zionism on college campuses and in cities throughout the United States and across the globe. Many protestors have openly supported Hamas and call for the total destruction of Israel. Some

---

56. Psalm 122:6.

demonstrations have turned hostile and violent with signs that proclaim, "Gas the Jews," and other odious rhetoric and actions.

These actions have shocked Jewish communities in America and elsewhere, and convince many people—Jews and non-Jews alike—that there is no distinction between antisemitism and anti-Zionism. Many Jews in the Diaspora now openly ask if they are safe and secure living in communities that once seemed open and welcoming to them. A common refrain seen and heard on print and social media is, "Your Jewish friends are not okay!" As faithful neighbors, Latter-day Saints are encouraged to check in with their Jewish friends to see how they are doing and empathize with their fragile emotional state in these difficult times.

3

Beliefs in Common with Latter-day Saints

By Professor Shon Hopkin

As the description of Jewish beliefs above demonstrates, much within Jewish thought resonates deeply with Latter-day Saint beliefs. Before digging into important similarities, expressing two cautions is extremely important. First, Latter-day Saints often feel a kinship with Jews that may lead some to believe that Jewish beliefs will look more or less similar to those of Latter-day Saints, and that a conversation between a Latter-day Saint and a Jew will be a constant movement from one exciting discovery of shared beliefs to the next, ending in the joyous realization that both had already believed the same things without even realizing it. These Latter-day Saints may then be disappointed to find that their "imagined Jew" is a real, fully formed individual with feelings, beliefs, and practices of his or her own, including a rich set of religious views that defy easy comparisons. This discovery can potentially lead those learning of their Jewish neighbors to feel slightly betrayed. If that feeling occurs, I encourage Latter-day Saints to remember that true humility and charity seeks to understand others as they truly are. There is joy in discovering and exploring the great depth and variety of religious belief in Judaism, and that discovery will hopefully lead to warmer, healthier interactions with one's neighbors, valuing them and understanding them for who they are rather than seeking to interact with them simply to re-create them as one would wish them to be.

The second caution is connected to the first. This book and this series are designed to help Latter-day Saints be better neighbors and friends with those of other faiths, understanding others better with an eye toward standing together with them in matters of faith, supporting and defending them in times of need, and simply rejoicing in the mutual discovery of deep friendship. As with most other people, Jewish people are sensitive to expressions of friendship that mask other motives. Due to their challenging history of conflict with their Christian neighbors, a history that often included such dreadful things as forced baptisms, kidnapping of children to raise them as Christians, and intense pressures to convert, Jewish feelings regarding evangelization or proselytizing are often even more sensitive. Latter-day Saints are well known for their desire to preach the gospel to the entire world. This identity is important and even crucial to Latter-day Saints, and we do not need to give up those ideals. But Latter-day Saints do need to understand that their friendliness may at times be understood simply as a desire to convert.

As a Latter-day Saint, when I engage in interfaith dialogue, my two basic goals are (1) to understand the beliefs, viewpoints, and practices of the other and (2) to help the other understand my own beliefs. I feel joy and success at those moments when I have seen the world through the eyes of the other, recognizing why they view things the way that they do, and when they have seen the world through my eyes. This mutual discovery changes both participants in the dialogue in powerful ways without necessarily causing one to wish to change religious identities. More will be said about the differences in Latter-day Saint and Jewish attitudes to proselytization and conversion in later sections of this book.

God

The first major topic that Rabbi Diamond appropriately chooses to address is faith in God. In any interfaith dialogue, Latter-day Saints can appreciate the approach of others whose faith in God plays an organizing role in their worldviews and behaviors. That people of faith should better understand each other is particularly pressing in a world that increasingly downplays the importance of faith in God, that distrusts moral codes based on anything higher or older than the immediate concerns of humankind, or that doubts or denies the existence of the divine. Many types of dialogue can increase peace in the world, but discussions among people of faith are becoming more and more important in our increasingly secular world.

For most Jews, faith means a belief in one God, the God of the Hebrew Bible. Latter-day Saint scripture also affirms the oneness of God. As stated in the Book of Mormon, "This is the doctrine of Christ, and the only and true doctrine of the Father, and of the Son, and of the Holy Ghost, which is *one God*, without end."[1] As with many others in the world, Latter-day Saints do not struggle as those in ancient times did with questions regarding which competing god from which land would receive their allegiance. Nor do they need to worry about competing priorities of devotion in an ancient pantheon or group of competing gods. Members of the Church view the Father, the Son, and the Holy Spirit as completely united in purpose, mission, goal, and intent. As a Latter-day Saint, it is important to my faith and focus to recognize that the Godhead is not divided but is one. It is also important to recognize that Latter-day Saint views about God—both with respect to the existence of three separate and distinct beings in the Godhead and with respect to God's corporeality (that God has a physical body)—are distinctive from those of most Jews, Muslims, and other Christians. Those differences are as important to explore, which will be done in the next section, as are the similarities.

Notwithstanding real differences, the similarities of belief on this topic should not be understated. Latter-day Saint challenges with polytheism are similar to those facing their Jewish friends and have more to do with what might be considered modern-day idol worship. Those challenges have everything to do with where we look for our sources of peace, security, strength, and meaning. Fame, fortune, and compelling distractions compete for the loyalty of Latter-day Saint faith and attention and threaten to pull away from faith in God. Latter-day Saints do not struggle to know whether they should be devoted to the Father or to the Son or to whose ethical system they owe their allegiance. When I worship on Sunday as a Latter-day Saint, I would never pause to question whether I

---

1. 2 Nephi 31:21; emphasis added.

am showing allegiance to the Father or to the Son. They are one, and there is no competition of values or of purpose in my devotion to Them. But I do struggle to give my primary loyalties to God in the midst of a world that constantly threatens to pull my trust to things that will not provide lasting joy, strength, or comfort.

Rabbi Diamond's expression of Jewish views regarding God's nature is powerfully evocative for the Latter-day Saint mind and heart. We also affirm that God is both omniscient and omnipotent; indeed, *Lectures on Faith*, published during the years that the Church was in Kirtland, states that it is impossible to have faith unto salvation without a belief in these two attributes of God. Diamond mentions the importance of the Jewish understanding of God as King, Father, Shepherd, and more. All of these views of God are also important to Latter-day Saints, and this is an area in which Jewish and Latter-day Saint discussions could bear significant fruit, and where Latter-day Saint thought about God could be greatly enriched—not necessarily by concepts that do not exist in the restored gospel, but rather by concepts that are not as frequently discussed among Latter-day Saints. For most Latter-day Saints, the concept that is most often relied upon is the understanding of God as a loving father, one who nurtures, trains, teaches, protects, and guides as a tender father would. As Joseph Smith put it:

> While one portion of the human race is judging and condemning the other without mercy, the Great Parent of the universe looks upon the whole of the human family with a fatherly care and paternal regard; He views them as His offspring, and without any of those contracted feelings that influence the children of men, causes "His sun to rise on the evil and on the good, and sendeth rain on the just and on the unjust." (Matthew 5:45.)[2]

Discussions regarding what it means to view God as King, Warrior, or Shepherd could expand views on both sides of the discussion regarding God's nature and identity.

---

2. Joseph Smith, "History, 1838–1856, volume C-1 [2 November 1838–31 July 1842]," *The Joseph Smith Papers*, 1321, accessed May 10, 2020, https://www.josephsmith-papers.org/paper-summary/history-1838-1856-volume-c-1-2-november-1838-31-july-1842/495. Or, see *History of the Church* 4:595.

Diamond's description of God as the Mysterious One may at first appear to contradict joyous Latter-day Saint affirmations that God can and should be known by His children.[3] Although there are some important differences in approach, teachings of the Church also affirm the grandeur, awe, and glory of God that can be sensed through God's Spirit but that cannot be fully expressed or understood by mortals. As God states in Moses 1:5, "No man can behold all my works, except he behold all my glory; and no man can behold all my glory, and afterwards remain in the flesh on the earth." The Book of Mormon echoes that sentiment during Jesus's postmortal visit to the Nephites: "And no tongue can speak, neither can there be written by any man, neither can the hearts of men conceive so great and marvelous things as we both saw and heard Jesus speak; and no one can conceive of the joy which filled our souls at the time we heard him pray for us unto the Father."[4] As important as the ability to know God is to Latter-day Saints, can any of us truly believe that we are able to grasp the fulness of God's glory, dominion, and might? These truths are only dimly understood by any of us, and only when we are touched by the Spirit of God. Cultivating a sense of God's infinite grandeur, a glory that is not fully knowable for the mortal heart or mind, can increase human desire for heaven. That view, which can be shared between Jews and Latter-day Saints, will work not only to enhance our appreciation of God but also to increase our appreciation of God's children and creations.

Although we sometimes mean different things when expressing the biblical truth that humans are created in the image of God, this biblical passage is highly important to both Latter-day Saints and to Jews. Even most nonreligious or agnostic Jews would likely see in this statement an expression that ennobles humankind and that can lead to wiser and healthier viewpoints and choices. Although Latter-day Saints often use this phrase to emphasize that God has a physical body and the physical similarity between God and His children, that focus should not obscure the importance of the views that Diamond describes. Human conduct *should* mimic divine conduct, or *imitatio dei*. We should not view ourselves simply as random products of nature, as biological machines whose decisions are fully preconditioned by bodily

---

3. See John 17:3.
4. 3 Nephi 17:17.

needs and by a desire for self-preservation. Rather, Jews and Latter-day Saints together affirm that there is something divine in God's human creations and that our self-understanding should include an effort to comprehend God so that we can better comprehend ourselves. Indeed, this worldview can completely change the way that one views oneself and the world, encouraging holier, less-selfish behaviors that can improve human choice and action. We are created to be Godlike.

Although I've mentioned the importance of people of faith coming to better understanding and cooperation, it is also crucial to remember, as Diamond states, that "as with most matters of Jewish thought, we do well to speak of multiple Jewish views of God rather than one single Jewish perspective on the nature of God." It is rare to find someone identifying as a Latter-day Saint who does not also affirm the importance of faith in God, no matter the current status of her or his faith. For a variety of historical reasons, as Diamond has expressed, there is a much broader variety of Jewish faith expression found in the world, including agnostic and atheistic approaches. In a discussion between Latter-day Saints and Jews, it is useful to determine how the Jewish participants feel about faith in God. How important is faith in God in guiding daily choices and worldviews? Is God a distant, moral force or a present, guiding influence? Is God best understood through logic and reason, scripture, experience with the divine? Each answer will likely offer an avenue of fruitful discussion and understanding. Knowing to which, if any, main Jewish group your friend belongs will provide some important guidance in his or her religious views, but the answers of every individual may vary in important and significant ways. Navigating a discussion of such personal and important topics can be fraught with some risks but is also highly rewarding.

Messiah (*Mashiah*)

Rabbi Diamond's discussion of God flows logically to the topic of the covenant that God has made with His people before Diamond discusses the Messiah. For Latter-day Saints, however, it would be difficult to progress from the topic of God without turning immediately to a discussion of the Messiah. Similar differences in the order of topics as this book continues will reflect the different ways of thinking about these concepts by Jews and Latter-day Saints.

Latter-day Saint understandings of the Messiah (Hebrew *Mashiah*) mirror those of most other Christians and are possibly the most significant point of difference with their Jewish friends. Notwithstanding the Christian identification of Jesus as the Messiah as well as the Son of God, the traditional Jewish understanding of the Messiah does fit in many ways with the Christian view of Jesus's identity and role at the time of His Second Coming. Just as in Jewish tradition, the Messiah will indeed usher in a millennial era of peace and prosperity, ruling as king. Although Messianic expectations are not strong or prevalent among some branches of Judaism, most Jews maintain hope in a millennial age and act either through patient faith or through active social programs and scientific discovery to bring about that ideal time and condition. Jews and Latter-day Saints can rejoice together in this shared hope, expressed so beautifully by Isaiah and others. The way in which the millennial age will come about and what it will look like when it arrives can be a fruitful area of exploration and discussion between Latter-day Saints and Jews.

Covenant (*Berit*)

The Bible and restoration scriptures unitedly affirm that God is willing to enter into covenantal relationships with His creations. As Diamond has explained, the concept of covenant (Hebrew *berit*) frames the Jewish understanding of God's interactions with them over the course of history. This is also centrally true for Latter-day Saints. The Book of Mormon title page declares that one of the book's main purposes is to serve as a witness that God has not forgotten His covenants with His people. Latter-day Saints often focus on the making of personal covenants between the individual and God—at baptism, in the temple endowment, and in temple sealing ordinances. The importance of individual, personal covenant-making is not completely foreign to Jewish thinking, but Jews more often view themselves as a part of biblical covenants due to their membership in the broader Jewish community. The covenant exists independent of their acceptance or rejection of it rather than being something that must be renewed by each individual in her or his relationship with God. Latter-day Saints can fully agree that God does not forget His covenants and that His ancient promises to His people remain in force. The ordinances found in the Church give Church members the opportunity to personally accept their role and participation in God's covenantal community.

Rabbi Diamond begins this book with a brief and straightforward historical background that starts with the great patriarch Abraham. Where would Latter-day Saints start the story? Although Latter-day Saints view the covenant as first being made between God and His children prior to the creation of the world—and then being renewed with Adam, Enoch, Noah, and others prior to Abraham—beginning with Abraham also makes sense for Latter-day Saint readers. We also view Abraham as one of our primary ancestors, one that is shared with the Jewish people, whether members of the Church regard themselves as descended from Abraham directly through a lost lineage or adopted into that line. The biblical covenant that by far receives the most attention in the Church is the Abrahamic covenant, which frames and gives life to the covenants that Latter-day Saints make in the temple, particularly to the promises offered in the eternal marriage sealing ceremony. The book of Abraham further demonstrates the Latter-day Saint commitment to and fascination with Father Abraham.

Latter-day Saints also view Moses as occupying a central role in the history of God's covenant with His people. This importance is evidenced both by Joseph Smith's teachings known as the book of Moses as well as by the Latter-day Saint belief that Moses came to the Kirtland Temple in 1836 to bestow the keys of the gathering of Israel upon Joseph Smith and the newly organized Church. Latter-day Saints affirm that God revealed Himself to Moses at Sinai, providing the Mosaic covenant, the revelations contained in the Torah, and a model of prophetic leadership. More will be said regarding Moses's role in the section describing differences between Latter-day Saint and Jewish viewpoints.

The Jewish People and Peoplehood

Important differences do exist between Jewish and Latter-day Saint views of the Mosaic covenant, which will be discussed later, but Diamond's description of the "cycle of covenants" resonates with Latter-day Saints, who often discuss this concept in terms of dispensational cycles of apostasy and restoration. Additionally, Latter-day Saint views that God's covenant with the Jewish people remains in force are significantly different and more positive than those of some or many Christians. Prominent strands of Christian thought have viewed the ancient biblical covenants as being fulfilled in Jesus and superseded (or done away with) by Christianity. I personally have heard one Christian leader describe Jewish beliefs as old, worn-out, and irrelevant in the blazing joy of Christian faith, representing a prevalent Christian view that the Old Testament lacks relevance today besides as a repository for faith-building stories and a few prophecies about the end of times. These views certainly do not describe all of Christianity, and Latter-day Saints in particular sharply disagree. As Joseph Smith put it:

> The kingdom of God was set up on the earth from the days of Adam to the present time, whenever there has been a righteous man on earth unto whom God revealed His word and gave power and authority to administer in His name. And where there is a priest of God—a minister who has power and authority from God to administer in the ordinances of the gospel and officiate in the priesthood of God—there is the kingdom of God.[5]

God's covenantal choice of the house of Israel, including the Jewish people, remains in force and His promises to them will all be fulfilled.

Two other points of similarity regarding God's choice of the descendants of Israel (including the Jews) as a covenant people should be mentioned here. First, Latter-day Saints view themselves as either being adopted into the house of Israel through the making of sacred covenants, or as being part of the lost and scattered remnants of the various tribes of ancient Israel who were mixed among all nations and who lost a sense of their covenantal history over the course of the centuries. Although most Jews will likely not be inclined to accept this Latter-day Saint view and will find it somewhat strange and naïve, my experience is that many *will* be able to accept that this self-understanding is centrally important to Latter-day Saints. It will likely be helpful for Jews to recognize that this feeling of kinship that Latter-day Saints feel with them is sincere. Warmth toward someone perceived as a distant family member feels (and hopefully is) safer than kindness motivated by a desire to convert or to change the other.

---

5.   Joseph Smith, "Discourse, 22 January 1843, as Reported by Wilford Woodruff," *The Joseph Smith Papers*, 4, accessed October 12, 2020, https://www.josephsmithpapers. org/paper-summary/discourse-22-january-1843-as-reported-by-wilford-woodruff/1. Or, see *Teachings of the Prophet Joseph Smith*, 271.

Next, although the Church is relatively new, Latter-day Saints and their history exhibit some marked similarities to the Jewish people. These similarities include the sense that God has chosen the Latter-day Saints as His covenant people, that this covenant peoplehood requires them to care for each other's needs in ambitious ways, that their covenantal status is connected to some of their historical experiences of persecution, and that they have an obligation to be a light to the world. Persecution against the Latter-day Saints forced them to move from New York to Kirtland, Ohio; Independence, Missouri; and Nauvoo, Illinois. Their time in Missouri was infamously cut short by Governor Lilburn W. Boggs's Extermination Order that saw Latter-day Saint property and land looted and stolen while the Saints were forcibly driven from the state amid violent attacks. Their time in Illinois began to close when Joseph Smith was murdered by a mob while ostensibly under protection of the state, and completely ended under threat of violence as they abandoned their beautiful city Nauvoo (from the Hebrew word meaning "beautiful"), which at the time rivaled Chicago in size. The "Mormon exodus" led them approximately 1,300 miles across uninhabited wilderness to their "Promised Land," a location in the desolate Salt Lake basin where they hoped to finally be allowed to develop undisturbed. Their "modern Moses," Brigham Young, rejected the pull of California's beauty, recognizing that the Latter-day Saints would likely end up experiencing the same fate if they tried to occupy that space. Most Latter-day Saints with pioneer ancestry have their own stories of ways that their ancestors both suffered and were miraculously preserved as they were led to Utah. Each of the areas listed above can provide space for further discussion and may surprise Jews and Latter-day Saints with some of the similarities that are revealed.

Israel—The Land and the State

Although the concept is not often emphasized in current Church discussions, Restoration scriptures often proclaim the importance of the connection between covenants and land, a concept that was central in the Abrahamic covenant and that continues to be of high importance to most Jews. Promises abound in the Book of Mormon, Doctrine and Covenants, and elsewhere that God will grant His people a holy land. Those promises will be partially fulfilled prior to the Millennium but will be fully realized for the Jews and for all of God's covenant people during the millennial era of peace and after the final end and renewal of the world as a celestial home.

Jewish views of land and covenant logically rest on the status of biblical lands known today by the world as Israel and Palestine. As described by Rabbi Diamond, although there are significant and heated disagreements in Jewish circles about many topics regarding Israel, the importance of the land is one of the near-universal values shared by all Jewish peoples, whether religious or nonreligious. For both secular and religious Jews, history has demonstrated the essentiality of a place for Jews to be safe from apparently never-ending cycles of antisemitism that constantly threaten the fabric of Jewish existence. Biblical proclamations that God has granted the land to His people only strengthen the importance of the land for many religious Jews. Where do Latter-day Saints weigh in on the State of Israel?

Latter-day Saint views of the State of Israel show strong and consistent support for the land as a haven for the Jewish people, a position that is enhanced by modern prophetic confirmations that God's ancient covenants regarding the house of Israel remain in effect. Notwithstanding that strong support, Latter-day Saints mirror significant concerns and questions shared by many Jews concerning the status and treatment of the Palestinians and what democratic law should look like in a nation that shows a legally mandated preference for one particular people. Jews often strongly appreciate the discovery of Latter-day Saint support for Israel. The reality that Joseph Smith sent one of the Church's highest leaders, Orson Hyde, on the long and treacherous journey to Israel to dedicate the land for the return of the Jews—while the Church was still only in its infancy and was plagued by threats to its very existence in the United States—resonates deeply with most Jews. In his prayer, which some Latter-day Saints view as prophesying of the great twentieth-century gathering of the Jewish people to Israel, he pled "for the gathering together of Judah's scattered remnants" and asked God to "incline them [the Jews] to gather in upon this land" and to "constitute her as a distinct people and government." The importance of that early and continuing Latter-day support for the existence of Israel is physically symbolized by the existence of the large Orson Hyde Memorial Garden that the city of Jerusalem created on the Mount of Olives in 1979 near where Orson Hyde gave his prayer in 1841. Since 1841 Latter-day Saint prophets and Church leaders have offered numerous other prayers with a similar focus and intent. The existence of the majestic BYU Jerusalem Center on Mount Scopus is another physical testament to Latter-day Saint commitment to these biblical lands. Latter-day Saint readers of this book are encouraged to read Rabbi Diamond's poignant description of the extended and shocking violence that began on October 7, 2023, and to follow his plea to reach out to those who have been so deeply affected by these devastating and tragic events.

The World and the World to Come (*Olam Haba*)

When interacting with non-Orthodox Jews, Latter-day Saints may be surprised that concepts of soteriology,[6] a topic that is highly developed in most Christian faiths, are not of primary concern. The importance placed on the next life—resurrection (Hebrew *tehiyat ha-maytim*) and heavenly salvation—are more closely aligned when speaking with Orthodox Jews. Because their reading of the Hebrew Bible is heavily influenced by the New Testament, the Book of Mormon, and other Restoration scripture, Latter-day Saints are often not aware that the Hebrew Bible focuses little on issues of the world to come. Although the topic of the next life has been and continues to be important to some groups of Jews, and can serve as an important area of discussion for some, issues related to social justice and peace in this life resonate deeply with most Jews. Latter-day Saints, of course, are also deeply committed to acts of *tzedakah* (feeding the poor, caring for the needy, and reaching out to the downtrodden). In my interfaith dialogues with Jewish friends, learning of the efforts being taken by Jewish organizations and by The Church of Jesus Christ of Latter-day Saints, whether in humanitarian aid to the world or in caring for their own, creates an important sense of shared common ground.

Diversity of Thought

Rabbi Diamond's description of Jewish sects and movements demonstrates a significant difference between Latter-day Saints and Jews. It can feel disconcerting to confront the wide array and diversity of Jewish thought that has developed throughout the centuries. The central organization and leadership of the Church creates much higher levels of similarity in thought and expression among Latter-day Saints. That being said, it is important for

---

6. Salvation in the next life.

Latter-day Saints to remember that not all Latter-day Saints think exactly alike on a wide variety of issues. The views, beliefs, and understandings of one Latter-day Saint are simply the views of one, and they are not perfectly representative of all Latter-day Saints everywhere. Due in part to their lengthy historical experience, and due simply to human nature, Jewish friends will appreciate recognizing that their Latter-day Saint neighbors have come to their own beliefs and viewpoints individually and thoughtfully, and that they acknowledge that other Latter-day Saints might understand or explain concepts differently than they do. Latter-day Saints often are very proud of the "unity of the faith" and of practice that is exhibited by members of the Church. But freedom to reason for oneself, to seek after inspiration and understanding directly from God, and to choose for oneself—including the freedom to disagree—are also central tenets of Latter-day Saint faith that will resonate with most Jews.

4

Areas Where Latter-day Saint Beliefs Differ

By Professor Shon Hopkin

Healthy, effective interfaith dialogue exhibits similar characteristics to relationship-building in general. Often a lasting friendship will begin with both sides enthusiastically appreciating all that is similar between them and marveling at the goodness manifest in the new acquaintance, which is typically at least somewhat idealized. If a relationship, however, is based only on similarities and does not progress to an understanding of deep differences, then the friendship will likely be unhealthy for one or both parties and may quickly dissolve when challenges arise. As important as it is for interfaith dialogue to understand and build upon similarities, it is also crucial for both sides to be fully honest about true differences and to do the difficult work to try to understand why those differences exist and why the other party may view the world in ways that contrast so strongly with one's own beliefs. To gloss over these differences sets the relationship up for future failure.

God

Most Jews already view the traditional Christian understanding of the Trinity—that the Godhead is made up of three persons that are one in substance—as at least partially polytheistic.[1] Latter-day Saints, of course, depart further from this view held by many (but not all) Christians, instead declaring that God the Father, God the Son, and God the Spirit are indeed one in purpose, goal, and intent (one in heart) but that they are three separate beings.

Unlike most Jewish and Christian readings of the Hebrew Bible, current Latter-day Saint understandings identify the name *Elohim* with God the Father. They believe that the God of the Hebrew Bible—whose name is not uttered by Jews but is represented by the four letters Y-H-W-H, known by Jews as the "Tetragrammaton" (often translated as "LORD" in the King James Version and pronounced by most Christians as Jehovah)—is the being who descended to earth and was born as the mortal Messiah, Jesus. The Gospel of John supports this identification of Y-H-W-H with Jesus. For most Jews, as for many Christians, the traditional Christian teaching of the Trinity is very difficult to understand. Although most Jews are deeply loyal to teachings in the Hebrew Bible that there is only one God and would strongly disagree with the belief in three separate beings in the Godhead, the Latter-day Saint understanding that Jesus is a separate being from the Father and is truly God the Father's Son, rather than being the same substance as God the Father, may be at least more intelligible for those with whom you talk.

Other Latter-day Saint understandings that God the Father has an exalted body of flesh and bones (in other words, a belief in the "corporeal" nature of God) are also important to discuss, although they will be surprising to many. As with Christianity, Judaism has a long history of interpreting any verses in the Hebrew Bible that refer to God's face or hands as metaphors that help humans to talk about God. They typically interpret the phrase that humans are created "in the image of God" as referring to the human ability to exercise faith and rational thought and to choose behaviors of holiness. As an additional challenge, the absence of a Messianic view in Judaism in which God descends and becomes human further removes Jewish thinkers from connecting God with any type of humanlike, physical body.

Although many Jewish and Christian theologians view a belief that God has a body as primitive and naïve, there is much in both Hebrew Bible and New Testament thought that can support the Latter-day Saint approach.

---

1. A term indicating a belief in many gods.

When discussing these types of differing religious views in an interfaith dialogue, my goals are not to convince my dialogue partners that I am correct but rather to show that a rational human being could hold these views. I also hope to demonstrate why those views are important and helpful to me and how they influence my worldview in positive ways. Taken together, the Latter-day Saint view that God has an exalted, physical body is connected to the view that He truly did create us in His image, that we share crucial similarities with Him, and that we can become like Him in the next life. From a Latter-day Saint perspective, these views do not diminish God the Creator in the slightest, but they do ennoble God's children and give us a positive, encouraging view both of the benefits and importance of the human body and of physical experience, and of our potential future destiny.

Other Latter-day Saint views of the nature of God and humans diverge even further from traditional Jewish and Christian understandings and will feel foreign to most Jewish thinkers, particularly to those who are not focused on the next life. Although these views are less central in Latter-day Saint teachings, depending on the depth and length of the conversations they can be helpful for others in understanding the cohesive nature of Latter-day Saint thought regarding the identity and destiny of human beings in relation to God. Most Jews and non–Latter-day Saint Christians believe that God is eternal in nature but that all other beings and things were created out of nothing by God (called creation *ex nihilo*). Further, many interpret the three-fold exclamation of the angels in Isaiah 6 that God is "Holy, Holy, Holy" as indicating that God is "wholly other" or completely and utterly different from humans. (Although Latter-day Saints agree that God is infinitely higher than human beings, they would not express God's nature as "wholly other.")

Joseph Smith instead taught that elements (that from which the world, the cosmos, and human bodies are made) and intelligence (that from which the human spirit is primarily made) are eternal and that God created or brought things into being by organizing them out of chaos. He is thus the creator of all things, but Latter-day Saints would also affirm that there is a core of humankind (indeed of all things) that is co-eternal with God. God is literally the Father or Creator/Organizer of the spirits of humankind, who lived with Him prior to their birth into this life. In a premortal council and conflict in which God presented His plan of salvation for His children, those of God's spirit children who accepted His plan were given the opportunity to be born on earth. By exercising faith they could return to live with the Father after their mortal life, becoming like Him, with a fully exalted, physical body.

Further, just as God is considered "wholly other" in most Jewish and Christian thought, beings such as angels and demons are also understood as completely different types of beings from humans. For Latter-day Saints, however, those of Heavenly Father's spirit children who rejected the plan presented in the premortal council were cast from heaven and became Satan and his followers (often called devils or demons). In a sense, Latter-day Saints view God, humans, angels (God's spirit children who have not yet been born on earth or the righteous who have already lived and died), and even demons or devils (those who were cast out of heaven and who lost their opportunity for salvation) as part of God's family, those who were initially created with the opportunity of becoming Godlike.

Again, these concepts may be helpful to discuss, but Latter-day Saint views about the nature of God and of humans will feel foreign to most Jewish thinkers, and even more so because they will not have encountered these ideas even in their conversations with other Christians. Although they may appear strange to Jewish dialogue partners, explaining why those viewpoints are helpful to Latter-day Saints will allow others to recognize why a Latter-day Saint might choose to believe this way. These teachings provide a cohesive view of heaven and earth, the nature of God and humans, and God's purposes for creating the earth. Although they differ from traditional Jewish and Christian thought, they do not inherently conflict with biblical teachings. One area of potential Jewish connection with the concept of a premortal existence may be found in the medieval, mystical teachings known as *Kabbalah*, which Rabbi Diamond has mentioned and which will be discussed further below. In part, the *Kabbalah* teaches that the goodness that emanated from God shattered in a premortal time and that the Jewish people are called to gather these scattered remnants of light through acts of goodness and charity so that God can be known again.

There are other areas in which Latter-day Saint views of God's plan of salvation for humankind fit more closely with Jewish thinking than with most Christian thought. Like most Jews, Latter-day Saints view the Fall as bringing about both the incredibly difficult and incredibly positive conditions of mortal life. This means that, like many Jews, they have a strong view of human agency in the exercise of free will. Both Latter-day Saints and Jews tend to be uncomfortable with the teachings of some Christians that all people are born with a stain of guilt from Adam's sin (known as original sin) or that humankind is born in a completely depraved or wicked state because of the Fall.

Messiah (*Mashiah*)

For most Jews, the reality that Jesus's life did not produce the expected physical or political freedom from Roman bondage is clear evidence that He could not have been the long-awaited Messiah. Latter-day Saints instead share the Messianic views of most other Christians. This, of course, means that their understanding of the Messiah is that Jesus came in the meridian of time to conquer sin and death and that He will return prior to the Millennium to reign upon the earth and initiate an era of peace and tranquility. At one point Joseph Smith said, "The fundamental principles of our religion are the testimony of the Apostles and Prophets, concerning Jesus Christ, that He died, was buried, and rose again the third day, and ascended into heaven; and all other things which pertain to our religion are only appendages to it."[2]

The Book of Mormon describes a group of Israelites who left Jerusalem about six hundred years before the birth of Jesus and travelled to the Americas. These Israelites had revelations that clarified the identity of the Messiah and emphasized that the God of the Hebrew Bible Himself—Y-H-W-H, known mortally as Jesus—would descend and be born as a human. They interpreted Hebrew prophets and law of Moses ordinances or rituals as teaching of and pointing to the nature and identity of the coming Messiah, whose mortal life would be one of suffering and sacrifice but whose second coming would be characterized by visible glory and power. Over time, these Israelites buried their scriptural records and lost their tribal memory of their Israelite identity. Joseph Smith was led many centuries later to their buried record and translated it by the power of God, providing the Book of Mormon. More will be said in the next section regarding Latter-day Saint views of Jesus and the Mosaic covenant, but the teachings of the Book of Mormon further influence Latter-day Saint understandings of the centuries prior to

---

2. Joseph Smith, "History, 1838–1856, volume B-1 [1 September 1834–2 November 1838]," *The Joseph Smith Papers*, 796, accessed October 12, 2020, https://www.josephsmithpapers.org/paper-summary/history-1838-1856-volume-b-1-1-september-1834-2-november-1838/250. Or, see *Teachings of the Prophet Joseph Smith*, 121.

Jesus's birth. They emphasize that some Israelites clearly understood Jesus's Messianic identity prior to His birth.

As in the previous section, a further discussion of Latter-day Saint Messianic understandings may be unnecessary depending on the length and depth of the conversation, but they may help Jews understand some of the reasons traditional Christians at times label Latter-day Saints as non-Christians. Latter-day Saints understand Jesus (equated with Y-H-W-H) both as having a core of "intelligence"—as with all spirits—that is co-eternal in nature with God the Father (equated with Elohim) but also as the firstborn spirit child of God premortally created/organized, and as having absolute pre-eminence among all of God's spirit children. They also view Jesus as the only begotten child of God the Father into mortality, the only of God's spirit children who was also God's physical, mortal child, born miraculously through virgin birth to Mary. Because these views differ markedly from traditional Christian Trinitarian views, they are heavily suspect to many other Christians. These teachings also help explain why Latter-day Saints will sometimes choose to describe Jesus as their "elder brother," even as they know Him as the Son of God, Y-H-W-H, the second member of the Godhead and the God of the Hebrew Bible.

Prophets, Covenants, and Missionary Work

As mentioned above, Latter-day Saints understand Moses as holding a high and important place in God's plans for His covenant people, but their understanding of Moses's prophetic roles differs somewhat from the Jewish conception that typically views Moses as the most important of all of the prophets, the one who gave the law of Moses that still defines Jewish self-understanding today. For Latter-day Saints, Moses—the greatest of the prophets until John the Baptist and Jesus—demonstrates how God always intends to work with His people, through the leadership of prophets who have the ability to communicate with Him. They view the cycle of the restoration of covenants as one in which prophetic leadership is lost and regained as God reinitiates His covenant promises. For Latter-day Saints, then, Moses was a crucial part of this covenant renewal following the loss of leadership that gradually occurred after Joseph in Egypt. Samuel played a similar role after a chaotic time in the reign of the Judges, and Jesus stepped into the role of restorer when He began His ministry. Joseph Smith is understood as taking a restoration role in modern times, restating God's covenant promises that had always remained in effect and helping bring faith in those promises back to life for those who would become Latter-day Saints. The Book of Mormon, the first scripture given by Joseph Smith as the translation of an ancient record of a lost branch of Israelites, affirms the same message. For Latter-day Saints, when God spoke to Moses on Sinai, He was following His ancient pattern of renewing covenant, revealing Himself to His prophet and providing new scriptural guidance as He communicated again with His people. Latter-day Saints also believe that God desires that each of His covenant children experience the prophetic gift and learn to communicate directly with Him. As Moses put it, "Would God that all the Lord's people were prophets, and that the Lord would put his spirit upon them!"[3]

Notwithstanding the high regard given to Moses, unlike most Jews the Book of Mormon and other Latter-day Saint teachings prioritize the Abrahamic covenant over the Mosaic covenant, as is also found in Paul's New Testament thinking. The Abrahamic covenant is itself a reiteration of the grand premortal covenant made first during the council in heaven, and later reaffirmed (possibly with different details being emphasized) with Adam, Enoch, Noah, and others; it remains in force and describes God's plan to bless and save His creations through covenant. Certain elements of the Mosaic covenant, however, are understood as being uniquely suited to the situation of the Israelites at the time and as being fulfilled in the atoning sacrifice of Jesus Christ. According to the Latter-day Saint view, the intricate sacrificial system, for example, was created in part with the intent to point toward and prepare for the ultimate atoning sacrifice of Jesus the Messiah. Most Jews would strongly disagree that the law of Moses has been fulfilled in Christ. For many it still forms the core of their covenantal self-understanding today.

Where does this place Latter-day Saints with *supersessionism*, the view held by many Christians that the covenants of the Hebrew Bible and the identity of the Jews have been superseded (replaced) by Christ and no longer have any meaning? The Book of Mormon and Latter-day Saints strongly affirm that God's covenant promises still rest with the house of Israel through the Abrahamic covenant and that all of His promises to them will be fulfilled. They view the Jews as one of the tribes of Israel. Latter-day Saint prophecy and belief affirm that they will be gathered back to the lands of

---

3. Numbers 11:29.

their inheritance. Latter-day Saints believe that the Jews have played and will continue to play a crucial and positive role under the Abrahamic covenant. Additionally, although they believe that the Mosaic covenant was fulfilled in Jesus, they believe that God was its author and that it thus contains powerful eternal truths—including but not limited to the Ten Commandments—that remain in force and that can continue to teach humankind about the mind, will, and nature of God.

For a variety of reasons that will be discussed later, most Jews are uncomfortable with Christian proselytizing or evangelization. Most Jews do not believe that they should encourage others to convert to Judaism, believing that Jewish practices were given by God specifically for the Jewish people and that God did not intend for all humankind to practice them. It is important for Latter-day Saints and their Jewish friends to recognize that Jews occupy a unique place in the Latter-day Saint approach to missionary work. On the one hand, Latter-day Saints do believe that at some point all of God's children will need to accept Jesus as the Messiah. Their efforts at missionary work are designed to follow the New Testament injunction to preach the gospel to all people.[4] For Latter-day Saints this includes both encouraging others to believe in Jesus Christ and helping them to gain an understanding that the prophetic role has been restored with modern-day prophets in The Church of Jesus Christ of Latter-day Saints. Notwithstanding their missionary identity, however, Latter-day Saints believe that the darkly negative historical impact of traditional Christianity upon the Jews pushes them strongly away from an acceptance of Jesus's Messianic identity. Although there have been brief efforts by Latter-day Saints to share Christian beliefs with Jewish people, Latter-day Saints have most often believed that the destiny of the Jewish people is in the hands of God and that the Jewish people have an important and positive role to play in the continued working out of God's plans with humankind. Latter-day Saints also believe that eventually, whether in this life or the next (as will be described in the next section), whether before, during, or after the Second Coming of Jesus, the Jews will be in a position to accept the Messianic role of Jesus.

Latter-day Saint teachings do mirror other Christian interpretations of biblical prophecies that anticipate a future event in which Jesus will descend upon the Mount of Olives to be recognized and accepted as the Messiah

---

4. See Mark 16:15.

by a group of His covenant Jewish people gathered there. Although these views may be offensive to Jewish dialogue participants, Latter-day Saints can affirm that they strongly believe in allowing full freedom to all to choose their own religious viewpoints without any compulsion, that they have deep respect for the dignity of all human beings as children of God, and that they have a unique respect and appreciation for the position that the Jewish people occupy in the former, current, and future plans of God.

As an additional but important aside, it should be mentioned that as part of the agreement to build the BYU Jerusalem Center, the Church signed an agreement that there would be no proselytizing in any way in Israel and that the BYU Center would not be used to evangelize others. Not only has the Church strictly maintained its side of that agreement, but the international nature of the Church and of modern mobility has influenced any missionary interactions that might occur between Latter-day Saints and Jews around the world. It is not fully impossible for a Jewish person living outside of Israel to be evangelized and to join the Church, but it is an unusual occurrence. More will be said about this topic in the section on Latter-day Saint historical engagement with the Jews.

This World and the World to Come (*Olam Haba*)

Although many Jewish dialogue participants may be less interested in Latter-day Saint soteriological views,[5] it is probably important that they understand some of the concepts that make the Church's teachings different from those of other Christian faiths. The belief in a premortal existence in which God's spirit children accepted God's plan, including an acceptance of the role of Jesus as Messiah, has already been mentioned. With this view, earth life becomes an opportunity to learn to become more Godlike, to live by faith in God, and to make choices that prepare for the next life. Love, friendship, commitment, service, selflessness, an appreciation for the human body and for human experience within healthy limits, an appreciation for family life, and a desire to be a light to the world all characterize Latter-day Saint views of a life richly and happily lived, notwithstanding severe tests and trials that come to many.

---

5. Beliefs about salvation in the next life.

Different religious peoples have differing ways to understand the reality that relatively few will accept religious truths that they believe are centrally important. Some Christians believe that anyone who does not accept Jesus during this life will be doomed to hell. Others believe that the requirement to accept Jesus cannot realistically be required by a loving, just God and that God will therefore save according to His understanding of the human heart. For many Jewish people, there is a particular role that is required of them as God's covenant people that necessitates their acceptance of the unique beliefs and practices found in the law of Moses, but the rest of humanity is required only to follow the seven laws that Jewish tradition says God gave to Noah, which basically require them to worship God and to treat others with justice.

Two important and unique beliefs—the belief in the spirit world and the belief in heavenly degrees of glory—cause Latter-day Saints to approach this challenging topic differently than most Jews or Christians. It will likely be helpful to explain these concepts clearly to Jewish acquaintances because Latter-day Saint claims to be members of the "only true and living Church"[6] can feel offensive and judgmental to others. These two concepts, however, demonstrate how Latter-day Saints can maintain a belief in the truthfulness of their church's teachings and at the same time can refrain from judging those who are not members of their church. First, unlike most Jews and other Christians, Latter-day Saints believe in a destination between death and the physical resurrection known to them as the spirit world. In the spirit world, all are given a full opportunity to recognize and accept truths that were not available to them during mortality. This belief allows Latter-day Saints both to believe that all (Latter-day Saints and everyone) can only enter heaven if they are willing to accept truth as it really is, but at the same time to withhold judgment on those they interact with during their lives who view things differently. Although the Church makes strong truth claims, Latter-day Saints are aware that all have a wide set of differing circumstances and that God will judge all according to those circumstances and will give all the opportunities missed in mortality. Latter-day Saints do not believe that they know who will be in heaven based simply on appearances during mortality, nor do they believe that a simple rejection of what they understand as truth can be easily understood as indicating the state of

---

6.   Doctrine and Covenants 1:30.

another's heart before God. In other words, Latter-day Saints would expect that many in their own Church may not be in heaven, while many who strongly disagree with them during this life might end up there instead. The concept of a spirit world allows Latter-day Saints to be more patient, more hopeful, and less judgmental with the great variety of belief they see throughout the world, including—and maybe most importantly—in their own families.

This belief also provides context for Latter-day Saint baptisms for the dead that are performed in their temples. As many Jews know, this practice has at times been a highly sensitive topic between Jews and Latter-day Saints. Latter-day Saints perform these baptisms in order to offer that blessing to those who did not have the chance to receive it in this life. It is considered a free offering to those who have passed away, not something that is forced upon those who are in the spirit world. Latter-day Saints do not believe that these baptism rituals automatically make others Latter-day Saints; rather, they perform the ordinances for those who may wish to accept them but who were unable to do so during mortality.

For some Jews, of course, any mention of a Jewish name in connection with a Christian baptism may bring up bitter historical memories of forced conversions in medieval times. To make matters worse, Jewish attention to genealogy means that the identities of those who have passed away are more easily available to Latter-day Saints who may be doing their own genealogical research. Careless and overenthusiastic Latter-day Saints have even done baptisms for the dead with names found on Holocaust lists, creating serious offense and demonstrating an unintentional but significant lack of sensitivity. The Church has worked hard to improve their ability and oversight to make sure that this culturally insensitive and inappropriate practice never occurs again. They have also emphasized that doing baptisms for the dead is intended as a way to provide blessings for one's own ancestors, rather than for those who are completely disconnected genealogically.

Another unique Latter-day Saint belief modifies the traditional Jewish and Christian understanding of heaven and hell as simple opposites with all "good people" going to heaven and all "bad people" going to hell. Joseph Smith taught of a vision in which he learned that all would be blessed in heaven according to what they had become, and that therefore heaven and hell were not simple opposites, but rather there would be "degrees of glory" in heaven, with hell or "outer darkness" reserved only for those who completely and fully rejected God after gaining a full knowledge of Him. This view of heaven nears universalism and emphasizes that God accepts and rewards all efforts at goodness throughout the world. Latter-day Saints are not surprised to find goodness and truth spread liberally through the world among all people and religious groups, and they will not be surprised to find the varying levels of goodness found in the world represented by degrees of glory in the afterlife.

5

Latter-day Saint "Holy Envy" of Jewish Beliefs

By Professor Shon Hopkin

In 1985, while defending The Church of Jesus Christ of Latter-day Saints against opposition to plans to build a new temple in Stockholm, Swedish New Testament scholar Krister Stendahl provided three guidelines for healthy interfaith understanding: first, to ask the believers of a religion what they believe rather than asking their enemies; second, to not compare the best in one's own religion to the worst in that of the other; and third, to leave room for "holy envy." With the third guideline, Stendahl was encouraging his listeners to find something in the religion of the other that they deeply admired, even to the degree of wishing that it might be found in their own religion. The interfaith encouragement to leave room for holy envy has resonated deeply with many and is often mentioned as an important part of interfaith discussions. Accordingly, this book and book series will also spend time and space "leaving room for holy envy."

As a Latter-day Saint, when I approach the teachings of Jewish sages and teachers, both modern and ancient, I am overwhelmed by the depth of thinking represented by such figures as Saadia Gaon, Judah Halevi, Maimonides, the *Baal Shem Tov*, Moses Mendelssohn, Theodore Herzl, Martin Buber,

Leo Baeck, Abraham Joshua Heschel, and Mordecai Kaplan. This brief list does not even begin to scratch the surface. The Jewish people have dealt with the full spectrum of human experience over the centuries, from power and influence to intense and prolonged persecution leading to mass murders and destruction. Over the course of centuries of religious hopes and promises that appear to many to still await fulfillment, Jewish thinkers have wrestled with what their suffering might teach them about the existence and nature of God and about His relationship with all of His creations and with the Jewish people in particular. This thought ranges at times from the pessimistic and gloomy to the patient and enduring to the optimistic and even boldly ambitious. For a people to endure the twentieth century Holocaust, as well as the millions of other violent deaths and the violent oppression that the Jews have faced again and again over the centuries, and to emerge still searching for meaning and victory in life does not occur without a remarkable resilience of spirit and depth of thought. It is difficult not to stand in awe at the millennia-long evidence of vast Jewish accomplishment, strength, and genius. High percentages of Jewish representation in the fields of technology, medicine, politics, and entertainment demonstrate the remarkable strength and resilience of Jewish approaches and intelligence.

Two short ancient examples of the strength and profundity of Jewish thought have influenced me perhaps even more than others. I was introduced to the teachings of Hillel the Elder as I began to study Mishnah and Talmud, two ancient sources of Jewish ethics and wisdom. Hillel is quoted and cited extensively in both works, but two of his statements have been popular for many and continue to stand out for me. The first is an expression of what has come to be known as the golden rule: "That which is hateful to you, do not do to your fellow. That is the whole Torah; the rest is explanation; go and learn."[1] The simplicity and generosity of this expression is inspiring, particularly as it pushes back against stereotypes of Jewish thinking (and especially Christian views of ancient Jewish thinking) as dangerously rules-bound. Hillel's injunction also demonstrates the "this-life" nature of much Jewish theology. For Hillel, the entire Torah is about not doing damage to others but treating them with respect and gentility, providing others the same consideration one would offer to oneself. I agree with Hillel, and, as a Christian, find his approach to mirror that of Jesus in the

---

1. *Babylonian Talmud*, Shabbat 31a.

New Testament: "Therefore all things whatsoever ye would that men should do to you, do ye even so to them: for this is the law and the prophets."[2] The teaching resonates deeply with me and draws me toward a deeper study and a more nuanced understanding of Jewish thought than that which I encounter in often one-sided Christian depictions.

The second famous statement by Hillel, one that has strongly influenced my daily attitudes and helped me be a more courageous person, is, "If I am not for myself, who will be for me? If I am only for myself, what am I? And if not now, when?"[3] Pushing against the self-effacing tendency to put our own needs even lower than the needs of others in the name of service or sacrifice or goodness, this statement reminds me that the greatest good is often found when we remain self-aware and sensitive to our own needs. I do not help others when I cause myself to disappear or abase myself below others, nor am I able to serve successfully when I ignore the kind of wisdom that allows me to move forward in healthy ways. Jesus's second great commandment asks no more than this: "Love thy neighbor *as thyself.*"[4] But if we only care for and about ourselves, and our self-awareness does not also lead us to look out for others, what does our existence mean or what value does it have? That which is simply self-preserving will only perpetuate one individual, and we all exist in connection with others. Jesus also taught, "A new commandment I give unto you, that ye love one another as I have loved you,"[5] elevating the teaching to "love thy neighbor" to the level of loving one's neighbor *as God loves.* Finally, the most important part of the statement, and one that I have repeated as a mantra to myself day after day when trying to make healthy choices and then maintain them, is, "If not now, when?" Now is the only time I can control, the only time that I can influence. For most decisions, there is no time that can be more successful than right now.

To jump to modern teachers, Rabbi Lord Jonathan Sacks, the former Chief Rabbi of the United Hebrew Congregations of the Commonwealth (United Kingdom), has had a strong voice and influence for me and many others. I will again mention just two of his statements in order to give a sense of his warm religious wisdom. The first demonstrates the type of religious curiosity and seeking that is highly important for Latter-day Saint

---

2. Matthew 7:12.
3. *Pirkei Avot* 1:14, translated by Charles Taylor.
4. Matthew 22:39; emphasis added.
5. John 13:34.

self-identity: "To ask is to believe that somewhere there is an answer. . . . We ask not because we doubt but because we believe."[6] I hope that Latter-day Saints continue to be question makers and answer seekers as modeled by their first prophet, Joseph Smith. One of the things I have most loved when I study with Jews is their bold willingness to question viewpoints, to seek for greater understanding, and to push—hard, sometimes—to improve knowledge. This is an area Latter-day Saints would do well to emulate.

The second statement by Rabbi Sacks builds on Rabbi Diamond's discussion of *imitatio dei*, the idea that humans are created in the image of God and that we must mirror Him and His goodness, particularly in the areas of compassion.

> Greatness, even for God, certainly for us, is not to be above people but to be with them, hearing their silent cry, sharing their distress, bringing comfort to the distressed and dignity to the deprived. The message of the Hebrew Bible is that civilizations survive not by strength but by how they respond to the weak; not by wealth but by how they care for the poor; not by power but by their concern for the powerless. What renders a culture invulnerable is the compassion it shows to the vulnerable.[7]

If I understand the God of the Hebrew Bible and the system of ethics that He provided in the Mosaic covenant and through His prophetic messengers, then I will recognize God as the being who desires to suffer with and care for the weak. When a group, religion, or individual loses a sense of that value, they are doomed to failure.

Another area of holy envy for me is much that is found within the Jewish mystical understanding known as *Kabbalah*, although it is important for Latter-day Saints to distinguish between Americanized expressions of *Kabbalah* found in pop culture and the authentic Jewish expression of *Kabbalah*. Just as the Latter-day Saint plan of salvation provides powerful motivation for faith, service, and courage and a framework for understanding the relationship between humankind and God, so does *Kabbalah* offer a powerful and uplifting worldview for Jewish believers. *Kabbalah* declares

---

6. *The Jonathan Sacks Haggadah* (Jerusalem: Koren Publishers, 2013), 106.
7. *To Heal a Fractured World* (New York City: Schoken Books, 2007), 37.

that the goodness emanating from God shattered in a time before the creation of the earth. That goodness and light is found spread throughout the world, and the goal of *Kabbalah* is to find the goodness, to recognize it, and to gather it back together. The method is to act as a light to the world by engaging in acts of goodness and kindness that heal the world from its initial break, a repairing process known as *tikkun olam.* This worldview encourages Jews to seek in a positive way to appreciate the goodness that they find in others, to battle injustice, and to engage in acts of kindness even when their immediate results are not obvious. *Kabbalah* includes a complex but beautiful set of views that describe the relationship between God and humans and that encourage worshipers into mystical communion with the *Ein Sof,* the Endless One. I have holy envy of many of the beliefs and practices of *Kabbalah.*

SECTION 2
Jewish Practices

6

General Overview of Jewish Practices

By Rabbi Mark S. Diamond

Prayer

Daily prayers are fundamental components of Jewish religious practice. Observant Jews pray three times each day in worship services known as *shaharit* (morning), *minha* (afternoon), and *ma'ariv* (evening). The weekday shaharit service is the longest of the three daily worship services and includes:

- Preliminary prayers and psalms;
- Prayers to acknowledge God's role in creation, redemption, and revelation, including the *shema*;[1]
- The *amidah*,[2] the heart of the liturgy with nineteen blessings of praise, petition, and thanksgiving recited in each of the three daily services;

---

1. Literally "hear"; a declaration of faith in one God from Deuteronomy 6:4.
2. Literally "standing."

- Prayers of supplication;
- A Torah service on Mondays and Thursdays during which three short Torah passages from the weekly lectionary cycle[3] are read aloud;
- Closing prayers, including a prayer of adoration and a special memorial prayer recited by those in mourning.

Jewish men wear a set of special religious symbols in prayer. A *kippah*,[4] or *yarmulka*,[5] is a small cap that is worn on the head as a sign of devotion to God. Observant Jewish men wear a *kippah* throughout the day, while others wear one when praying, studying, and/or eating a meal. *Kippot*[6] come in different sizes, colors, and fabrics, but all serve the same purpose of honoring God. Latter-day Saints may also notice that many Orthodox Jewish men wear hats in addition to or instead of a *kippah*. Some Jewish men choose to wear a baseball-style cap in public and a more traditional *kippah* in prayer and study.

During morning worship services, Jewish men also wear a *tallit*[7] with four corners and fringes to reflect the law found in Numbers 15:37–41 to put fringes on the corners of one's garments. Adult Jewish males wear a *tallit* at virtually all morning services, including *Shabbat* and festivals, throughout the year. As with *kippot, tallitot*[8] come in a variety of styles, colors, and fabrics. All have four sets of fringes and serve the same purpose: to remind the wearer to remember and observe God's commandments.

Yet another symbol of Jewish prayer is called *tefillin*.[9] These are two leather boxes that contain small pieces of parchment with Torah verses that command placing signs upon one's hand and head. Attached to each box are black leather straps that are either wound around the arm and hand (the hand *tefillin*) or dangle in front of the chest (the head *tefillin*). Jewish men recite blessings as they place the *tefillin* on their forehead, arm, and hand during weekday morning services.

---

3. A fixed pattern in which the entire Five Books of Moses are read publicly in synagogue in a one-year or three-year cycle.
4. Hebrew for "cap."
5. Yiddish for "cap."
6. Plural of *kippah*.
7. Prayer shawl.
8. Plural of *tallit*.
9. Phylacteries.

Kippah, tallit, and *tefillin* are traditional symbols worn by Jewish men. In contexts in which Jewish women and men share equal religious roles, women may wear some or all of these symbols to demonstrate their religious equality with their male counterparts. In Orthodox Jewish communities, Jewish boys and men wear a special ritual undergarment called a *tallit katan.*[10] This enables them to fulfill the biblical commandment to put fringes on their four-cornered garments, even when styles have changed and most shirts no longer have corners. Those who wear a *tallit katan* either tuck the fringes inside their clothing or leave them dangling outside, a familiar sight in traditional Jewish settings. Jewish males do not wear a special prayer shawl (*tallit*) during morning worship before the age of thirteen, or, in the case of many Orthodox communities, before marriage.

In Judaism, prayer is not reserved for worship services alone. Jewish tradition prescribes a comprehensive set of blessings for many occasions, especially eating. There are special blessings recited before consuming fruits, vegetables, grain products, and every other food. Traditional Jews recite *berakhot*[11] before and after meals and typically being a meal with the blessing called ha-motzi[12] over bread. Blessing bread before a meal replaces individual blessings over other foods. Blessings are also recited after a meal. The longer version is called birkat ha-mazon[13] and is recited after a meal at which bread has been eaten; a shorter version is recited after meals and snacks without bread.

The Sabbath (*Shabbat*)[14]

The concept of a day of rest—*Shabbat* (Sabbath)—may well be the greatest gift the Torah bestowed upon the Jewish people and the world at large.

---

10. Literally "small *tallit.*"
11. Blessings.
12. Literally "he who brings forth."
13. Literally "blessing of the food."
14. Much of this material is quoted and adapted from Mark Diamond's chapter, "Shabbat in Jewish Thought and Practice," in *Understanding Covenants and Communities: Jews and Latter-day Saints in Dialogue,* ed. Mark S. Diamond and Andrew C. Reed (Provo, UT: Religious Studies Center, Brigham Young University; New York: Central Conference of American Rabbis Press, 2020), 195–226. The author acknowledges with appreciation permission to do so from the Central Conference of American Rabbis and the Religious Studies Center, Brigham Young University.

In an oft-quoted reflection on the tradition of the Sabbath, essayist Ahad Ha'am[15] wrote: "More than Jews have kept Shabbat, Shabbat has kept the Jews." Throughout history, allegiance to the laws and customs of *Shabbat* has been a prime indicator of traditional Jewish identity.

The institution of a weekly day of rest derives from several biblical passages, including the creation narrative and the Ten Commandments:

The heaven and the earth were finished, and all their array. On the seventh day God finished the work that He had been doing, and He ceased (rested) on the seventh day from all the work that He had done. And God blessed the seventh day and declared it holy, because on it God ceased from all the work of creation that He had done.[16]

Remember the Sabbath day and keep it holy. Six days you shall labor and do all your work, but the seventh day is a Sabbath of the Lord, your God: you shall not do any work—you, your son or daughter, your male or female slave, or your cattle, or the stranger who is within your settlements. For in six days the Lord made heaven and earth and sea, and all that is in them, and He rested on the seventh day; therefore the Lord blessed the Sabbath day and hallowed it.[17]

These biblical verses set forth the theological and practical implications of the day of rest. Jews are bidden to rest on the Sabbath because God rested on the seventh day *and* because God freed the Israelites from bondage in Egypt. Free men and women may refrain from work on the Sabbath, a luxury not afforded to slaves who are subject to their master's commands and schedule. Having been redeemed from servitude, the truly free human being becomes a servant of God and thereby obeys the divine command to keep the Sabbath.

Faithful observance of the Sabbath laws assumes a unique role in biblical Israel and among observant Jews thereafter. Specific mention is made in the Torah of labors prohibited on Shabbat—plowing, harvesting, kindling a fire, gathering food or wood.[18] The sages of the rabbinic tradition expanded

---

15. "One of the people"; the pen name of Asher Tzvi Hirsch Ginsberg.
16. Genesis 2:1–3, Jewish Publication Society (JPS) translation.
17. Exodus 20:8–11, JPS translation.
18. Exodus 34:21, 35:3, 16:29–30; Numbers 15:32–36.

this list by deriving thirty-nine *melahot*[19] associated with the preparation and construction of the portable tabernacle of Israelite worship. These *melahot* may be grouped into two broad categories—acts of exploiting nature and acts of creating or improving upon matter. Any work that involves even the most minute form of creating, improving, or destroying an object is prohibited according to traditional Jewish law. This clarifies why *Shabbat*-observant Jews, to this very day, adhere to Sabbath restrictions that seem to bear little relation to common explanations of what constitutes work.

Jewish tradition also highlights the positive, joyful aspects of Sabbath observance. *Shabbat* home rituals—including meals with special foods, candle lighting, family blessings, prayers over wine and *hallah*,[20] table songs, *birkat ha-mazon*, and *havdalah*[21]—serve to reinforce bonds with family and friends and enhance the Sabbath experience. Synagogue rituals—additional prayers on Friday evening and Saturday, the public reading of passages from Torah and Prophets (*haftarah*), and a sermon on the weekly scriptural portion—serve to strengthen communal bonds and collective allegiance to norms of prayer, learning, and observance. Sabbath rest and renewal are nourished by other time-honored *Shabbat* activities—reading, taking a nap, strolling through the neighborhood, playing games with family and friends, enjoying the outdoors, and appreciating moments of peace and quiet that nurture the mind, body, and spirit.

In times of relentless persecution and intolerance, in conditions of extreme poverty and suffering, Jews sought refuge in the simple, quiet joys of a Sabbath of peace and harmony. On *Shabbat*, Jews were transformed from endangered subjects of church and state to the noblest of royalty. The loneliness of weekday living gave way to the hopes and dreams of husbands and wives wedded to one another, to their God, and to the holy *Shabbat*. In Jewish households wherein couples struggled to put food on the table six days a week, somehow the *Shabbat* table glowed with a special spice—a favorite food reserved for the Sabbath, a loaf of *hallah*, a pot of *cholent*[22] with a treasured piece of meat or two. "Sabbath queen" and "Sabbath bride" are two beloved images from the Jewish prayer book that are enduring metaphors for the holiness and mystery of Shabbat.

---

19. Proscribed activities.
20. Braided egg bread.
21. "Separation"; blessings over wine, spices, and a braided candle to conclude *Shabbat*.
22. Sabbath stew.

The Jewish Calendar

The weekly institution of a holy day of rest is supplemented by an array of annual holy days and holidays in the Jewish faith tradition. Historically, the Jewish calendar precedes the familiar Gregorian calendar and is based on the lunar cycle with twelve months of either twenty-nine or thirty days. This calendar is intercalated (adjusted) to the solar calendar by adding an extra month seven times in a regular nineteen-year cycle. These Jewish leap years ensure that festivals remain linked to their respective seasons and helps to explain why Jewish holidays may fall "early" or "late" on the Gregorian calendar. The first sliver of the new moon marks *Rosh Hodesh* (the new month), itself a minor holiday marked by the addition of extra prayers in the daily liturgy. In recent years, groups of Jewish women have reintroduced a venerable custom of celebrating *Rosh Hodesh* as a special women's holiday.

The Jewish day begins in the evening at sunset and continues through the following evening. This practice is derived from the language of the creation narrative, "And there was evening, and there was morning."[23] Traditional Jews usher in *Shabbat* and all other holy days with prayer services in their synagogues and the lighting of candles, family blessings, prayers over wine and bread, ritual washing of hands, table hymns, and grace after the meal in their homes. Although certain Sabbath restrictions are lessened on other holy days, they too are full days of rest and observant Jews refrain from work on these festivals.

Holy Days

Three Jewish holy days—Passover, *Shavuot*, and *Sukkot*—are known collectively as the three pilgrimage festivals. In ancient Israel, people journeyed to Jerusalem to celebrate these festivals with sacrifices at the Temple. Later Jewish tradition imbued these holidays with agricultural, historical, and spiritual layers of meaning.

Passover is observed for seven days in Israel and by Reform Jews around the world. Traditional Jews in the Diaspora add an eighth day of Passover due to a potential confusion of dates in ancient times. Prior to the standardization of the Jewish calendar in the fourth century, witnesses reported

---

23. Genesis 1.

the first sighting of the new moon to the Sanhedrin,[24] and the court's proclamation of the new month had to travel by messengers from one town to another. Diaspora communities might receive the announcement after considerable delay, and of necessity they added an extra day to major holy days as a religious "insurance policy." This practice endures among observant Diaspora Jews in modern times, with an additional day added to the pilgrimage festivals of Passover, *Shavuot*, and *Sukkot*.

Passover, known as *Pesah* in Hebrew, is the spring harvest festival and begins on the fifteenth day of the Jewish month of *Nisan*.[25] This beloved holiday celebrates the liberation of the Israelite slaves from servitude in ancient Egypt. Harking back to biblical commandments, traditional Jews refrain from eating *hametz*[26] for the entirety of the holiday. Instead, Jews eat *matzah*[27] and celebrate the festival at a *Passover seder* in their homes. Each of the foods on the special *seder* plate symbolizes the bitterness of slavery, the sweet taste of redemptive freedom, or the joyful renewal of life each spring. Family and friends come together at the *seder* to enjoy a festive meal and retell the narrative of the exodus from Egypt in poetry, prose, and song, with unique customs designed to retain the interest of children throughout the evening. The *seder* text, known as a *haggadah*,[28] has been printed in thousands of different editions, from magnificent illuminated manuscripts to paperback versions published by Maxwell House to contemporary adaptions with focused themes of modern-day slavery, liberation, redemption, and renewal.

Shavuot[29] is the late-spring harvest festival and is held on the seventh day of the month of Sivan,[30] seven weeks after the first day of Passover. While it was solely an agricultural festival in biblical days, *Shavuot* took on major significance in later Jewish tradition as the season of the giving of Torah. Many Jews devote a portion of the holiday to the study of Torah and other sacred Jewish texts; some even stay up all night engaged in intensive Jewish learning. This custom revives a Jewish mystical practice called *tikkun leyl*

---

24. Jewish High Court.
25. The first month on the biblical calendar.
26. Leavened products.
27. Unleavened bread.
28. Telling.
29. Literally "weeks"; known as Pentecost in Christian tradition.
30. The third month on the biblical calendar.

Shavuot[31] that harks back to the belief that a person should not sleep on the night when they will hear the voice of God in the morning.[32]

Sukkot[33] is the fall harvest festival and begins on the fifteenth day of the Jewish month of *Tishrei*.[34] It is a seven-day holiday, with an eighth day called *Shemini Atzeret*[35] added both in Israel and the Diaspora. A ninth day called *Simhat Torah*[36] is added to *Shemini Atzeret* by traditional Jews in the Diaspora.

Sukkot is an especially colorful holiday highlighted by rich symbolism and imagery. Many Jews build *sukkot*[37] to recall the booths the Israelites dwelt in on their long journey from Egypt to the Promised Land, as well as the booths farmers construct as temporary shelters during harvest season. Some Jews eat, dwell, and sleep in their *sukkot* for seven days; others eat some or all of their meals in the *sukkah* during the holiday. These temporary huts serve as potent symbols of the frailty and fragility of life.

Jews also take up symbolic plants and fruits to mark the *Sukkot* holiday. An *etrog*[38] and *lulav*[39] are waved each of the seven days of the festival in a choreographed ritual that reminds us that God is found everywhere in the universe. Of the three pilgrimage holidays, *Sukkot* is the festival that retains much of its agricultural imagery and brings Jews back to a simpler life and a keen appreciation of the natural world.

Shemini Atzeret is alternately viewed as the eighth day of the *Sukkot* festival or a separate holiday in and of itself. The sages of the rabbinic tradition share a lovely metaphor to explain why there is yet another holiday after a full seven-day festival. God, we are told, is like a human monarch whose children, grandchildren, and other relatives gather together to celebrate the festival with their extended family. The celebration is so festive and memorable that the monarch tells his relatives to remain for another day to enhance

---

31. Literally "correction on the night of *Shavuot*."
32. See the commentary of the twelfth century sage Rabbi Abraham ibn Ezra on Exodus 19:11.
33. Literally "booths"; known as tabernacles in the Christian tradition.
34. The seventh month on the biblical calendar.
35. Literally "the Eighth Day of Assembly."
36. Literally "The joy of Torah."
37. Temporary booths or huts adjoining their homes.
38. Citron.
39. Palm branch bound with myrtle and willow leaves.

and extend the joy of the holiday. And so it is that *Shemini Atzeret* comes to preserve the Jewish season of joyful reunion for another day.

In Israel and in Reform Jewish congregations, *Shemini Atzeret* is combined with *Simhat Torah*; traditional Jews observe *Simhat Torah* as a separate holiday, the ninth day of this busy festival season. *Shemini Atzeret* has only a few special rituals to mark the day, including the recitation of a prayer for rain in the liturgy. *Simhat Torah*, by contrast, has numerous customs to celebrate the completion of the annual lectionary cycle. On this holiday, Jews gather in synagogue for the public reading of the last passages of the Book of Deuteronomy (the end of the Torah) and the first passages of the Book of Genesis (the beginning of the Torah). The congregation's Torah scrolls are removed from the Holy Ark and worshipers carry them in seven joyous circuits around the synagogue. Children walk along with their parents and wave simple flags to reflect the joy of the occasion. In the morning worship service in Orthodox synagogues, each male Jew is afforded the opportunity to ascend the *bimah*[40] to recite blessings before and after the public reading of a scriptural passage. In congregations that have equal religious roles for men and women, all adult Jews are invited to participate in this *ritual,* known as an *aliyah.*[41]

Passover, *Shavuot*, and *Sukkot* were the preeminent holy days in ancient Israel. While they are still widely observed today, the high holy days of *Rosh Hashanah* and *Yom Kippur* bring the largest number of Jews to synagogue services. *Rosh Hashanah*[42] is held on the first and second days of *Tishrei*[43] and marks the beginning of the new Jewish year. Reform Jews generally celebrate one day of this festival rather than two days. Worship services are held in synagogues in the evening and daytime, with special sets of prayers, scriptural readings, and sermons added to the prayer services.

Rosh Hashanah begins a ten-day period of introspection, reflection, and self-assessment known as *aseret yamei teshuvah.*[44] Jews are bidden to carefully examine their words and deeds over the past twelve months, repent of their transgressions, and vow to do better in the new year. The *Rosh Hashanah*

---

40. Raised platform or altar.
41. Literally "ascent" or "Torah honor."
42. Literally "Head of the Year."
43. The seventh month on the biblical calendar; commonly referred to today as the first month due to the celebration of *Rosh Hashanah*.
44. The Ten Days of Repentance.

liturgy (prayers) portrays God as a divine shepherd with a Book of Life awaiting the recording of the names of all persons who pass before Him seeking judgment. During these ten Days of Awe, God will decide our fate for the coming year. Three acts, we are told, may avert the severity of the decree—repentance, prayer, and *tzedakah*.[45]

The preeminent symbol of *Rosh Hashanah* is the *shofar*,[46] which is sounded in the synagogue at various points in the liturgy. The blasts of the *shofar* serve as a Jewish alarm clock, a piercing call to worshipers gathered in synagogue to assume responsibility for their shortcomings and (re)turn to God and to righteous conduct in the new year. In Jewish homes, *Rosh Hashanah* is marked by festive meals with favorite foods and apples dipped in honey as family and friends wish one another a good and sweet new year. Many Jews visit a local river or stream during the holiday and cast small pieces of bread into the water. This ritual, known as *tashlikh*,[47] is a symbolic mode of removing one's sins and starting the new year with a clean slate of deeds.

Yom Kippur, the Day of Atonement, falls on the tenth day of *Tishrei* and completes this solemn season of the Jewish calendar. Jews eat a meal before the holy day begins in the evening and then commence a full fast until the next evening. Observant Jews refrain from eating and drinking for the duration of the fast, designed to focus their energy and attention on spiritual matters. There is one other full fast day each year on the Jewish calendar— *Tisha B'Av*,[48] which commemorates the destruction of both the First Temple and Second Temple in Jerusalem.

On *Yom Kippur*, large numbers of Jews congregate in synagogues for *Kol Nidre*,[49] the evening worship service. Special confessional prayers are inserted into the evening and daytime orders of prayer, and extra worship services reflect the solemnity and urgency of the holiest day of the year. Some Jews spend the entire day of *Yom Kippur* in their synagogues engaged in prayer. After the fast day ends, Jews return to their homes for a festive

---

45. Literally "righteous giving."
46. Ram's horn.
47. Literally "casting."
48. Literally "the ninth day of the month of *Av*."
49. Literally "all vows."

break-fast meal with relatives and friends. Soon thereafter, they begin preparations for the *Sukkot* holiday that begins only four nights after the close of *Yom Kippur*.

Holidays and Commemorations

Rosh Hashanah, Yom Kippur, Passover, *Shavuot, Sukkot, Shemini Atzeret,* and *Simhat Torah* are all holy days on the Jewish calendar. Traditional Jews observe them as days of rest, though the seven-day Passover and *Sukkot* festivals have full days of rest at the beginning and end and semiholidays known as *Hol Hamo'ed*[50] in between. Two additional festivals—*Hanukkah* and *Purim*—are joyous holidays that are not days of rest on the Jewish calendar. *Hanukkah* begins on the twenty-fifth day of the month of Kislev[51] and concludes on the second day of the month of Tevet.[52] This eight-day festival celebrates the second century BCE victory of the Maccabees over their Greco-Syrian adversaries. According to rabbinic tradition, the Maccabees recaptured the defiled Temple in Jerusalem, found only one cruse of pure oil, and rekindled the temple *menorah*[53] to mark their victory. The oil should have kept the menorah's flame lit for only one day, but a miracle occurred and the *menorah* lights continued to burn for eight full days. To commemorate this miracle, Jews light special *Hanukkah menorahs* in their homes and synagogues for eight nights, adding an additional light each evening. The young and the young at heart look forward to receiving presents, playing games, and eating favorite foods for the duration of the holiday.

The holiday of *Purim*[54] is found in the book of Esther and falls each spring on the fourteenth day of the Jewish month of Adar.[55] The biblical narrative tells the story of the Jewish queen Esther who outwits the evil advisor (Haman) to a blundering Persian monarch (Ahasuerus) and averts an impending disaster for her people. *Purim* is an especially colorful fun-filled holiday with costumes for children and adults, synagogue services filled with the loud sounds of noisemakers to drown out the name of the villain in

---

50. Literally "the secular in the festival."
51. The ninth month on the biblical calendar.
52. The tenth month on the biblical calendar.
53. Candelabrum.
54. Literally "lots."
55. The eleventh month of the Jewish calendar.

the public reading of *megillat Esther*,[56] and *Purim* skits designed to poke fun at rabbis, teachers, and most everyone else in the community.

Modern rabbis have added several additional observances to the Jewish calendar. *Yom HaShoah* (Holocaust Day), the twenty-seventh day of *Nisan*, marks the revolt of Polish Jews in the Warsaw Ghetto and commemorates the slaughter of six million Jews at the hands of the Nazis and their henchmen. *Yom HaZikaron* (Memorial Day), the fourth day of the Jewish month of *Iyar*,[57] commemorates the men and women who fell in defense of the State of Israel and is observed both in Israel and the Jewish Diaspora. *Yom Ha-Atzma'ut* (Independence Day), the fifth day of *Iyar*, marks the founding of the Jewish state, when David Ben Gurion and other Zionist leaders met in Tel Aviv in May 1948 to declare Israel an independent nation. *Yom Yerushalayim* (Jerusalem Day), the twenty-eighth day of *Iyar*, is an Israeli national holiday that celebrates the reunification of the city of Jerusalem during Israel's Six-Day War in June 1967.

Dietary Laws (Kashrut)

The Torah lays the groundwork for the practice of *kashrut*, the Jewish dietary laws. *Kosher* means "fit" or "proper," and the biblical mandate to keep kosher rests on the idea that God commands Jews to fill their daily lives with holiness in eating foods, the most basic of human needs. For Jews who observe the dietary laws today, keeping kosher entails the following:

1. Abstaining from unclean species, including pork products and shellfish;
2. Eating meat only from clean animals (cattle, sheep, and others) that have been slaughtered in a ritual manner and drained of blood;
3. Avoiding any mixture of milk and meat products in food preparation or consuming milk and meat products at the same meal;
4. Maintaining separate sets of dairy and meat pots and pans, utensils, dishware, and so on to ensure complete separation of milk and meat products.

---

56. The Scroll of Esther.
57. The second month on the biblical calendar.

Jews who keep kosher carefully check labels when they shop to ensure that the foods they buy are certified as kosher by reputable religious authorities. Latter-day Saints may notice some of these labels—OU, Circle K, Triangle K, CRC, and many others—when they purchase prepared food products. These labels are registered trademarks of national or international kosher certifying bodies, whose *mashgihim*[58] ensure that nonkosher ingredients are not used in the preparation of these products. Some products are labeled as dairy, others as meat, and many others as *pareve*,[59] neither dairy-based nor meat-based that may be used as an ingredient for either meat or dairy recipes or served alongside dairy or meat meals. Common *pareve* foods include kosher fish (species of fish with fins and scales), fruits, vegetables, rice, pasta, nondairy breads, and spices.

Jews observe the detailed kosher laws to varying degrees of strictness and rabbinic authority. Some only eat meat that has been slaughtered by certain *shohtim*[60] approved by their rabbi. Others accept as kosher any meat with proper kosher certification. Many Orthodox Jews do not eat in nonkosher restaurants; other Jews may eat cold foods such as salads in these restaurants; still others may eat fish or dairy products (but not meat) in nonkosher establishments. Many Jews do not observe the dietary laws at all. For Latter-day Saints, this array of kosher practices can be confusing and disconcerting when they extend hospitality to their Jewish neighbors by sharing foods and inviting their neighbors to meals. The author offers this piece of advice to Latter-day Saints: ask beforehand what level of kosher observance their neighbors adhere to prior to extending meal invitations or bringing foods to their neighbors' homes.

The Life Cycle: Birth

Jewish tradition provides customs and guidelines to mark life transitions from birth to death. These rituals instill life's joyous and sad moments with deep spiritual significance. Life-cycle events are opportunities for individuals and their families and communities to celebrate and commemorate milestones and comfort and console one another in times of trial and loss.

---

58. Kosher inspectors.
59. Literally "neutral."
60. Ritual slaughterers.

The birth of a baby is marked by rituals that are observed in the home or the synagogue. A Jewish boy is ritually circumcised on the eighth day after birth, following the practice established by the patriarch Abraham in the Torah.[61] This practice is known as a *berit milah*[62] or a bris.[63] A *mohel*[64] performs the ceremony in the presence of parents, relatives, and friends. The baby boy receives his Hebrew name in the *berit milah* ceremony, a name he will henceforth be called by in the synagogue and other Jewish religious contexts.

Baby girls receive their Hebrew names either in a synagogue ceremony or in a set of rituals in the home. In Orthodox Jewish settings, the father of the baby receives an *aliyah*[65] in synagogue on the Sabbath following her birth, after which blessings are recited for the mother's health and the baby girl is formally named. In egalitarian Jewish settings, both mother and father may receive a joint *aliyah* or another honor on the *bimah* and have their daughter named in this manner. Increasingly, Jewish couples opt to have a home ceremony known as *simhat bat*[66] or *berit bat*[67] to denote full equality of boys and girls in Jewish religious practice. These ceremonies mimic *berit milah* ceremonies with similar prayers and rituals, save for the actual circumcision procedure and the eighth-day requirement. As with a *berit milah*, a baby girl receives her Hebrew name during these home ceremonies.

Pidyon ha-ben, literally "redemption of the son," is a ritual that Jews celebrate to mark the birth of a firstborn son. The theological foundations of this *mitzvah* are found in the Torah:

> And you must redeem every first-born male among your children. (Exodus 13:13)

> The first issue of the womb of every being, man or beast, that is offered to the Lord, shall be yours; but you shall have the first-born of man redeemed. . . . Take as their redemption price, from the

---

61. Genesis 17:9, 12.
62. Literally "the covenant of circumcision."
63. Literally "covenant."
64. Either a certified specialist in the practice of Jewish ritual circumcision or a physician skilled in both the medical and religious procedures.
65. Literally "going up"; the honor of blessing the Torah.
66. Literally "the joy of a daughter."
67. Literally "the covenant of a daughter."

age of one month up, the money equivalent of five shekels by the sanctuary weight. (Numbers 18:15–16)

In this age-old ceremony, the infant boy's parents (or father alone in a non-egalitarian context) redeem him from a *kohen* (priest) thirty-one days after his birth. *Pidyon ha-ben* is only done for baby boys who qualify as *peter rehem*, the first issue of the mother's womb. Nor is the ceremony done for sons who are of priestly or levitical descent, since they cannot be redeemed from service to God.

Bar Mitzvah and *Bat Mitzvah*

In Jewish legal tradition, boys reach the age of majority when they become thirteen years and one day old; girls reach the age of majority at twelve years and one day old. The ancient Jewish sages recognized that girls generally mature earlier than boys, a curious distinction in a male-dominated culture. According to Jewish law, when boys and girls become young adults, they are held responsible for their actions and are expected to follow the positive and negative commandments of Jewish law.

In the modern world, family and community mark these transitions from childhood to adulthood with a *bar mitzvah* or *bat mitzvah*. *Bar mitzvah*[68] is usually a synagogue-based ceremony in which a young man ascends the *bimah* and receives an *aliyah* during the Torah service. This may take place on any occasion when the Torah is read publicly—*Shabbat* morning, *Shabbat* afternoon, *Rosh Hodesh*, or a Monday or Thursday morning worship service. The *bar mitzvah* boy may do much more during the worship service—leading the congregation in prayers, chanting or reading one or more portions of the Torah, chanting the *haftarah*,[69] and/or delivering a short sermon. Parents, grandparents, and other relatives and friends are often given additional synagogue honors during the worship service, and parents may present their son with a *tallit*[70] and deliver brief remarks to him.

In congregations that have equal religious roles for men and women, the *bat mitzvah*[71] ceremony is identical to a bar mitzvah ceremony. While

---

68. Literally "subject to the commandment."
69. Additional portion from the prophets.
70. Prayer shawl.
71. Literally "daughter of a commandment."

some girls celebrate this ritual at age twelve, many communities delay the ceremony until age thirteen to align its timing with boys of the same age. As with a *bar mitzvah*, a *bat mitzvah* may lead some or all of the service, read from the Torah and/or *haftarah*, deliver a sermon, and so on. For boys and girls, the ceremony is followed by a festive meal to celebrate this milestone in the life of a young Jewish adult.

In recent years, there is a growing trend in some communities to hold *bar mitzvah* and *bat mitzvah* ceremonies in settings other than a synagogue. Some families prefer to celebrate this milestone at home, in a hotel, at a camp, or in another favored location. Parents may secure the services of a rabbi, cantor, or another knowledgeable Jewish individual to tutor their child, preside over the service, bring a Torah scroll, and arrange the ceremony to fit the needs of their son or daughter and invited guests.

In Orthodox settings, a girl's *bat mitzvah* is normally celebrated at age twelve, and gender-based ritual distinctions mandate that a *bat mitzvah* differ from a *bar mitzvah*. The young woman's father often leads some of the prayers and chants a Torah portion and/or a *haftarah* portion. The *bat mitzvah* may deliver a homily during or after the worship service. In some Orthodox settings, women will conduct a separate "women's only" *minyan*[72] that will allow a young woman to more closely align her *bat mitzvah* ceremony with its male equivalent.

For boys and girls, a "comprehensive" *bar mitzvah* and *bat mitzvah* ceremony represents a significant milestone in their Jewish learning and path to adult life. When they chant one or more portions from the Torah scroll, as is often the case in these ceremonies, they do so without the benefit of vowels, punctuation, or cantillation notes. This takes months and even years of Jewish schooling and meticulous preparation. Latter-day Saints can appreciate the religious spirit and educational efforts that combine to make the ceremony a genuine highlight in a young person's spiritual growth and development.

In some congregations, Jewish teenagers celebrate a confirmation ceremony, a life-cycle milestone early Reform rabbis adapted from Christian practice and tied to the Jewish festival of Shavuot with its theme of the giving and receiving of Torah. Originally, this was a replacement for the *bar mitzvah* ritual at age thirteen and a project to have young people affirm

---

72. Prayer quorum of ten.

their Jewish identity at a more mature age of fifteen or sixteen. Over time, the effort failed to eliminate the time-honored *bar mitzvah* ceremony. The contemporary outcome is a synagogue landscape in which many congregations offer only *bar mitzvah* and *bat mitzvah* ceremonies, while others hold out the "carrot" of confirmation for young adults who continue their Jewish education for several more years.

Conversion

Traditional interpretations of Jewish law define a Jew as one whose birth mother is Jewish, known as matrilineal descent. The Reform and Reconstructing Judaism movements also recognize the Jewish identity of one whose father is Jewish, known as patrilineal descent. All Jewish movements recognize individuals who formally embrace Judaism as converts or Jews-by-Choice. Traditionally, converts undergo a period of study of Jewish beliefs and practices, Hebrew language, and Jewish history, accompanied by experiential living of *Shabbat* and Jewish holidays.

Typically, potential converts appear before a *bet din*[73] of three rabbis who confirm their willingness to join the Jewish people and ask questions about their Jewish studies and practices. Male and female converts undergo immersion in a *mikveh* (ritual bath) to demarcate their non-Jewish and Jewish status. Following the *mikveh* ceremony, Jews-by-Choice are blessed with Hebrew names as the sons and daughters of the patriarch Abraham and matriarch Sarah.

In traditional Jewish movements, uncircumcised males who wish to become Jewish must have a *berit milah*, a major surgical procedure performed by a doctor with a rabbi or *mohel* present to recite the appropriate blessings. Males who were medically circumcised undergo *hatafat dam berit*[74] performed by a *mohel* or rabbi. This begins the conversion process that will be continued and completed with the rituals listed above.

Rabbis and Jewish movements differ in their respective conversion standards and rituals. Orthodox authorities frequently add a requirement that potential converts formally and fully embrace all matters of Jewish law, including strict adherence to the laws of *kashrut* and traditional observance of *Shabbat* and Jewish holy days. More liberal rabbis may wave traditional

---

73. Literally "law court."
74. Literally "taking a drop of covenantal blood."

conversion requirements of *berit milah* for men and *mikveh* and *bet din* for men and women. However, there is a clear mandate in Jewish tradition that whenever and however individuals become Jews-by-Choice, they are fully welcomed into the Jewish community. Indeed, many converts go on to assume key leadership roles in synagogues and other communal institutions, with some becoming rabbis, cantors, teachers, and professionals in Jewish organizational life.

Marriage

In Judaism, marriage is a sacred bond, and the traditional Jewish wedding ceremony reflects both the joy and sanctity of this important life transition. In days when couples married at a very young age, there were two distinct phases of marriage rituals—*kiddushin* or *erusin*[75] with the exchange of a ring or another object of value and the signing of a document, and *nisu'in*[76] with the couple coming together under a *huppah*,[77] the recitation of seven nuptial blessings, and other rituals. These two phases were often separated by a year or more, and the couple would only live together after they celebrated their wedding ceremony in the presence of family and community.

The modern Jewish wedding combines both of these steps into one ceremony, with the reading of a *ketubah*[78] to delineate the betrothal and the formal ceremony of marriage. Jewish weddings may be held in synagogues, hotels, gardens, or any site that the couple selects based on their needs and wishes. A rabbi or cantor often officiates at the wedding ceremony, completes and signs the Jewish and civil documents of marriage, and guides the couple through the steps of the wedding.

In a typical Jewish marriage ceremony, both the bride and groom are escorted to the *huppah*[79] by their respective parents. The bride may circle the groom up to seven times as the ceremony begins, a symbol of his new role in her life. In ceremonies that reflect equal roles for women and men, the bride and groom may circle each other at the outset of the wedding.

---

75. Betrothal.
76. Nuptials.
77. Marriage canopy.
78. Jewish marriage document.
79. Marriage canopy.

The traditional wedding rituals include prayers of welcome and a betrothal blessing recited over a cup of wine that the couple share. Next the groom presents a ring to his bride and recites a traditional phrase that affirms the betrothal "according to the laws and traditions of Moses and the people of Israel." The bride often presents a ring to the groom and recites a similar phrase to him in marriage ceremonies marked by equal roles for men and women.

The wedding officiant then reads all or part of the *ketubah*[80] and shares a brief message with the couple. The ceremony continues with the recitation or chanting of *sheva berakhot*, seven nuptial blessings, after which the couple shares a second cup of wine. The officiant continues by affirming that the wedding ceremony has been conducted in conformity with Jewish tradition and the laws of the appropriate state or commonwealth. Often the couple receives a closing blessing, the priestly benediction found in Numbers 24:24–26. As the final act of the wedding ritual, a small wrapped glass is placed on the floor and shattered when the groom steps on it (sometimes both groom and bride step on the glass). This act recalls the destruction of the holy Temple in Jerusalem and serves as a reminder that even in moments of great joy Jews are bidden to recall tragic events of Jewish history and strengthen their bonds to their people and heritage.

As with many Jewish beliefs and practices, Latter-day Saints may witness some or all of these rituals at Jewish weddings. Much depends on the preferences of the couple and their families and their respective levels of Jewish observance and affiliation. In non-Orthodox communities, single-sex wedding ceremonies are becoming more common as civil authorities certify these relationships as legal marriages.

The issue of marriage between a Jew and a non-Jew, known as intermarriage, is a complex one in Jewish life today. A 2013 Pew Research Center study, *A Portrait of Jewish Americans*, found that "44% of currently married Jewish respondents—and 58% of those who have married since 2005— indicate they are married to a non-Jewish spouse." The growing phenomenon of intermarriage in the Jewish community elicits an abundance of responses. Many authorities promote conversion of the non-Jewish spouse, welcome and integrate non-Jewish partners into synagogue life, and encourage intermarried couples to raise their children as Jews. More traditional

---

80. A Jewish marriage contract.

leaders sound an alarm and warn that rising rates of intermarriage imperil the Jewish future. Rabbis in the Orthodox and Conservative Jewish movements do not officiate at interfaith marriage ceremonies; many (but not all) Reform, Reconstructing Judaism, and other liberal rabbis will do so. Among rabbis who officiate at interfaith weddings, some will only officiate when a set of conditions is met, such as a pledge to raise offspring as Jews or a promise not to mix different religious traditions in the home.

Divorce

Marriage is viewed as a holy relationship that binds a couple together. When those bonds are broken and a divorce ensues, Jewish law mandates that the couple obtain a Jewish bill of divorce in addition to a civil dissolution of marriage. A *get*[81] is issued by a *bet din*[82] to certify that the partners are no longer married according to Jewish law. In the Diaspora, a *bet din* normally issues a *get* only after the couple has received a civil divorce.

In the Orthodox and Conservative Jewish movements, neither a divorced husband nor wife can remarry another Jewish person without obtaining a *get* to end the prior marriage according to religious law. Failure to obtain a *get* is a serious matter in traditional Jewish communities and has serious *halakhic*[83] consequences for any offspring born to a divorced woman and her second husband. While some Reform rabbis and rabbis in other liberal streams of Judaism do not mandate a *get* in cases of civil divorce, others do so in the spirit of Jewish unity and collegiality across denominational lines.

Death and Mourning

Two primary *mitzvot*[84] guide Jewish practices of death and mourning: *kevod ha-met*[85] and *nihum avaylim*.[86] When a Jew dies, the family and community traditionally honor the deceased by making immediate arrangements for the funeral and preparing the body for burial. Jews are generally

---

81. Jewish divorce document.
82. Jewish religious court.
83. Jewish legal.
84. Commandments; plural of *mitzvah*.
85. Honoring the deceased.
86. Comforting the mourners.

buried in special Jewish cemeteries where their loved ones and other community members have been laid to rest. Special Jewish funeral homes often are called upon to assist with funeral and burial arrangements.

In traditional Jewish circles, honoring the deceased includes the following rituals:

- Ritually washing the body and wrapping the corpse in simple *takhrikhin*.[87] These rituals are normally performed by members of a *hevra kaddisha*[88] in the funeral home.
- Reciting Psalms and "guarding" the body from the moment of death until the funeral. This *mitzvah*, called *shemira*,[89] may be performed by friends, relatives, or paid attendants.
- Placing the body in a simple, plain, wooden coffin. Jewish tradition stresses that all persons are equal in death, if not in life.
- Avoiding any unnecessary disturbances of the body, including embalming and autopsy, unless mandated by civil law. Cremation is highly discouraged in the Jewish tradition, especially in the aftermath of the Holocaust.

It is common practice for rabbis and/or cantors to conduct Jewish funeral and burial services. They include the recitation of Psalms, memorial prayers, and a eulogy or eulogies in honor of the deceased. The funeral service may be held in a memorial chapel, a synagogue, or at the gravesite. Friends and relatives may be invited to serve as pallbearers to accompany the casket from the funeral to the burial site.

The burial service itself is brief and usually includes Psalms, memorial prayers, and the recitation of the Mourner's *Kaddish*[90] by members of the immediate family. A common traditional custom is to invite relatives, friends, and others in attendance to place shovelfuls of earth on the casket after it has been lowered into the grave. This practice is a final act of love and reverence for the departed and symbolizes life's cycle of "dust to dust."

---

87. Linen shrouds.
88. Literally "holy society" or burial society.
89. Literally "watching" or "guarding."
90. A traditional Jewish prayer of mourning recited in a quorum of ten people.

Following the funeral and burial, mourners return to the family home to begin the observance of *shiva*,[91] the first of three successive periods of mourning. At this point relatives, friends, and community members shift their focus to comforting the mourners. A simple meal is set for mourners to eat upon returning home. For the first seven days, visitors come to the home to share remembrances of the deceased and bring comfort to family members who are mourning the loss of their loved one. Traditional customs during the *shiva* period include holding prayer services in the home to allow family members to recite the Mourner's *Kaddish* in the presence of a quorum of ten. In some homes, mirrors (a sign of vanity) are covered and mourners sit on low stools to reflect the disruption in their lives. They may wear a piece of clothing that has been torn, or a special torn ribbon, as a further sign of mourning.

Many people feel uncomfortable and ill at ease when they visit mourners who are "sitting *shiva*." This is understandable in a culture in which we use metaphors such as "memorial gardens" and "passing away" to soften the harsh reality of death. The author encourages Latter-day Saints and all visitors to share memories of the deceased and respect the solemnity of the mourning rituals when they visit a *shiva* home. These practices enable mourners to begin the lengthy process of healing after a loss.

Jewish tradition recognizes that it takes time to return to normal life after the death of a loved one. The first seven days of intense mourning are followed by an additional twenty-three days, which combined make up what is known as the *sheloshim* (thirty) period. Mourners return to their jobs or schools, continue to recite the Mourner's *Kaddish* daily or weekly, and traditionally refrain from enjoyable activities such as listening to music or watching movies. For children who have lost a parent, *sheloshim* leads to the third and final period of mourning, an additional ten months after the burial during which time they recite the Mourner's *Kaddish* on a regular basis to honor their parent's memory.

Additional mourning practices include the unveiling of a gravestone or marker at the burial site. This ceremony may take place at any time between one month and one year after the funeral and burial. Family members and friends gather at the cemetery to uncover the memorial marker, recite Psalms and prayers, and share remembrances of their departed loved one.

---

91. Literally "seven."

The anniversary of a person's death is known as a *yahrzeit* and is traditionally marked according to the date on the Jewish calendar. Traditional customs include the recitation of the Mourner's *Kaddish* at religious services on that date and making a donation of *tzedakah* to honor the deceased. Jews also honor the memories of their departed by coming to the synagogue for special *yizkor* (remembrance) prayer services on four holy days each year— *Yom Kippur, Shemini Atzeret,* and the last days of Passover and *Shavuot.*

As with other Jewish laws and customs, it is important to note that Jews have different levels of observance regarding the traditional laws of funerals, burials, and mourning practices. Many Jews follow the guidelines described above; others omit various funeral and burial customs; many others observe a less traditional form of mourning, such as a shorter *shiva* period. This diversity in mourning practices is yet another example of the variety of beliefs and practices in contemporary Jewish life.

7

Practices in Common with Latter-day Saints

By Professor Shon Hopkin

Although Latter-day Saints and Jews share some beliefs, the sense of shared values shines even more brightly in the area of religious practice. Many Christian faiths are heavily oriented to correct thought and belief. This orientation flows from a concern voiced in the apostle Paul's letters with being too "works oriented" and the fear that someone will engage in positive works with the belief that they can "earn" salvation or save themselves through their own righteousness. Although Latter-day Saints share some of these sensitivities and concerns (as do Jews), they have historically been very willing to heavily emphasize the importance of correct actions through following commandments (Hebrew *mitzvot*) that tell us how to live and that God requires us to follow. The temple recommend questions that all Latter-day Saints need to answer in order to participate in temple ordinances demonstrate attention to both correct thought and correct action (although both categories of the temple recommend questions allow for a wide variety of Latter-day Saint belief and behavior, focusing in on those things that are most essential to Latter-day Saint identity). The first three questions emphasize faith in God, Christ, and the restoration of the gospel.

The next question bridges the gap between belief and action, asking about the sustaining of Church leaders. Ten of the remaining questions emphasize actions such as honesty, sexual morality, tithing, living the Word of Wisdom, and other behaviors. (One question asks if those who are divorced are current in any assistance that may be due to their ex-spouse and to their children.) This is all to say that not only will Latter-day Saints find much in the Practices section that resonates with them, but they will also find the general emphasis and approach of Jewish religious practices to fit well with Latter-day Saint viewpoints regarding the importance of living God's commandments in order to obtain a happy and healthy life.

Prayer

Rabbi Diamond begins his discussion of Jewish practices with the human desire to communicate with the divine. There are significant differences between the typical patterns of Jewish and Latter-day Saint prayer (Hebrew *tefillah*). But the encouragement to seek after the divine in prayer reaches every corner of daily life and weekly worship for both traditions. Diamond mentions morning (*shaharit*), afternoon (*minha*), and evening (*ma'ariv*) prayers, along with prayers at the weekly Sabbath worship services and on holy days. Latter-day Saint prayer times show some similarity, with most Latter-day Saints emphasizing morning and evening prayers, prayers at mealtimes (known in Jewish practice as *birkat ha-mazon*, but said by Latter-day Saints using unprepared words rather than brief recitations), prayers during worship services, and numerous unprepared, informal prayers in times of need or of thanks. Latter-day Saints are commanded to "pray always";[1] most Latter-day Saints interpret this as an injunction to maintain a constant awareness of God's presence in their lives and to think and act in the full light of that connected awareness.

Although Jewish prayers most frequently repeat ideas and words from the scriptures or from other sages and teachers down through the centuries, while Latter-day Saint prayers show a strong preference for unprepared speech that is focused on immediate needs, the purposes for prayer are similar. Jews often give prayers to create a division (Hebrew *havdalah*) between sacred and profane (or worldly, nonsacred) time and to elevate what could be

---

1. 2 Nephi 32:9.

simple human or animal behaviors towards holiness. The morning prayers (*shaharit*) remind the Jewish worshipper that God is in charge of life and death, that He has in a sense preserved and renewed the life of the prayer after the unconsciousness of sleep, and that the day ahead should be lived in purposeful efforts at holiness. The short prayers Jews offer before eating (*ha-motzi*) are reminders that the food comes from God's bounty and would be impossible without Him; they designate what could be the routine filling of the belly or a greedy act of physical pleasure instead as something that celebrates earthly blessings and the joys of physical experience. Prayers during Jewish worship services similarly demarcate (or set apart) sacred time and experience from the regular activities of mortal life; they prepare the worshipper to enter into the Divine Presence.

These purposes all resonate with Latter-day Saints. Although Latter-day Saint prayers before meals often emphasize the petition for God to bless the food or the experience in some way, true efforts at prayer no matter the time or occasion petition God to sanctify human experiences and remind Latter-day Saints that they are in the hands of God and that they should seek to communicate with their loving Father even though they cannot see Him. Latter-day Saint prayers occur in a variety of settings: in private worship, family settings, public worship and other group settings, or ritual settings such as the sacred prayer of the sacrament or the united prayer of the temple endowment.

Latter-day Saints additionally have a long history of singing choral hymns. Unlike some of the singing in Jewish worship services, their congregational hymns typically contain significant amounts of harmonizing; the Tabernacle Choir at Temple Square is famed for their choral renditions. These songs are considered worshipful and united prayer by Latter-day Saints, and their enthusiasm can often be felt in their musical expressions, much as they can in Jewish worship services.

It is not an exaggeration to state that prayer is the religious behavior most often engaged in by both Jews and Latter-day Saints as a form of worship. Prayer gives meaning, shape, and form to the religious life and devotion of both peoples. The only other form of religious behavior that might compete with prayer in the importance of creating a truly religious life for both Jews and Latter-day Saints would be service (*tzedakah*), particularly when the charitable act is recognized as a service to God or a service to one of God's children.

Regarding the ritual clothing—*kippah*, *tallit*, and *tefillin*—often used by Jews in prayer, Latter-day Saint parallels are most clearly found within the boundaries of temple ordinances, which include sacred clothing. A Latter-day Saint attending a Jewish *Shabbat* service might be fascinated to see the the bags or briefcases that are used by some Jews to hold the *tallit* because they are similar to those that Latter-day Saints use for their temple ritual clothing. Additionally, the Latter-day Saint sacred undergarment that is first received in a temple ordinance and that is worn throughout the day and night is evocative of the *tallit katan*. As with the *tallit katan*, the temple garment serves as a reminder to Latter-day Saints of their covenantal identity and commitments, and of the Lord's promises to protect and to guide them.

The Sabbath (*Shabbat*)

Keeping the Sabbath day (*Shabbat*) holy (observed on Sunday by most Christians) has always been important to Latter-day Saints, but that focus has increased in recent years, with Church leaders identifying Sabbath-day observance as one of the practices that can most invigorate Latter-day Saint religious life. The renewed Sabbath emphasis has often pointed to Jewish practice and examples as a guide. All of the purposes of Sabbath worship mentioned by Rabbi Diamond have also been taught by Church leaders, with particular emphasis on the Sabbath as a day to worship God and as a day of rest. Although the idea of understanding the Sabbath as a celebration of freedom from servitude has received some attention, this idea is sometimes less frequently discussed in Latter-day Saint circles. The reminder that we are able to worship because we have been made free could be discussed more often among Latter-day Saints and could help motivate us to be more joyful and grateful in our Sabbath expressions, reducing feelings of constraint or compulsion in any self-imposed Sabbath day restrictions.

Unlike most religious Jews, Latter-day Saints do not have detailed commandments or restrictions that they believe God has required them to follow on the Sabbath, believing instead that the detailed Sabbath requirements of the Mosaic covenant have been fulfilled. They do believe, however, that God has commanded them to honor the Sabbath, and most Latter-day Saints believe that they should do so by following certain self-imposed restrictions and duties, similar to the Jewish concept of *melahot* that Rabbi Diamond mentioned above. Their Sabbath-day observance is thus more strictly practice-oriented than that of many other Christians. As with many observant Jews, Latter-day Saints do their best to refrain from labor or from other activities such as shopping or dining out that are not essential and that might cause others to labor. Lists of other Sabbath activities that many Latter-day Saints restrict on the Sabbath vary widely from home to home. These self-imposed restrictions demonstrate the Latter-day Saint desire to make the Sabbath a day that is set apart from other days. In distinction from observant Jews, most Latter-day Saints use electronics with relative freedom on the Sabbath, especially for religious purposes. Latter-day Saint worship services are typically full of phones or tablets being used to read along in the scriptures or to follow along in the hymns.

Many Jews attend worship services to welcome in the Sabbath on Friday evening and then return to Sabbath worship on Saturday morning. Together these worship services may take several hours, depending on the congregation. The Sabbath for most Latter-day Saints also includes participation in worship services, with a central focus on the ordinance or religious ritual known as the sacrament (which many other Christians refer to as the Eucharist). Sunday worship meetings typically last two hours and include singing, prayer, the ordinance of the sacrament, talks or devotional speeches given by members of the congregation, group study of scriptural texts, and planning for efforts in community service. In my interfaith activity with Jewish friends, attendance at each other's worship services has been joyful, connecting, and enlightening, helping each side to get a better sense for the rhythms of each other's religious life.

In addition to worship services, many Latter-day Saints also gather for family meals and family time (similar to Sabbath meals on Friday evening in Jewish homes), and many use this time to visit extended family, friends, or those in need. Many also use the extra time to do family history research (genealogy), another significant area of shared interest with Jews and Latter-day Saints, who see genealogical effort as a fulfillment of Malachi's promise that the hearts of the children will be turned to their fathers.[2] Although some, particularly children and teenagers, feel a sense of restriction on the Sabbath, the importance of joyful Sabbath activities is often emphasized and many adults find the Sabbath a crucial time of spiritual, emotional, and physical renewal, as is true for many Jews.

---

2. Malachi 4:6; Doctrine and Covenants 2:2.

Liturgy and Holy Days—Passover (*Pesah*), Day of Atonement (*Yom Kippur*), and Others

"Liturgy" describes a style of worship that follows a set schedule of readings, prayers, and religious ritual from Sabbath to Sabbath in a cycle that begins anew each year. The cycle of scripture readings, prayers, singing, and worship that characterize the progression of the Jewish liturgical year are mostly absent in Latter-day Saint life. Latter-day Saint worship more closely mirrors the lack of liturgical repetition that exists in many Protestant "low church" (less formalized) forms of worship than it does in the "high church" (more formalized) worship styles found in Roman Catholic, Eastern Orthodox, Anglican, and some other Protestant churches.

Besides the weekly worship services of the Sabbath, important dates for most Latter-day Saints include Easter and Christmas, with April 6 (the date of the official organization of the Church in 1830) and July 24, or Pioneer Day (which commemorates the entry of the early Church pioneers into the Salt Lake Valley following their long exodus from Nauvoo), also receiving honorable mention. Although these holidays, along with others such as Thanksgiving that depend on local culture and practice, receive attention in sacrament meeting talks, they still do not demonstrate the kind of liturgical worship patterns found in Jewish worship. Latter-day Saint worship does rotate with regularity around Church conferences, with two general conferences broadcast from Salt Lake City and featuring talks by key Church leaders occurring in early April and early October. As with Jewish attention to holy days, these are considered significant times of renewal. They are also times when modern prophets give inspired messages that provide leadership, direction, and guidance to the Church, in some ways like the Sabbath message given by a Jewish congregation's rabbi. These conferences may also include changes in Church practices that are understood by most Latter-day Saints as coming from God through revelation.

Mention should also be made of the monthly practice of fast Sunday. This special Sabbath occurs on the first Sunday of each month, echoing to a certain degree the New Month (*Rosh Hodesh*) in Judaism in its timing or the Day of Atonement (*Yom Kippur*) in its emphasis on fasting. For Latter-day Saints, fast Sunday includes, when physical limitations allow, a twenty-four hour fast from food and drink, accompanied by the monetary donation of a fast offering that should be as generous as possible but that should at least equal the cost of the missed meals. This offering is understood by Latter-day Saints as following Isaiah's prophetic guidance that fasting should help to "undo the heavy burdens and to let the oppressed go free."[3] It is used entirely to help feed and provide other assistance to those in the Latter-day Saint community who are in need. Jewish visitors to a Latter-day Saint sacrament meeting during a fast Sunday should be prepared to experience the monthly testimony meeting in which any member of the Latter-day Saint community can choose to stand and share expressions of faith and encouragement that are designed to strengthen and unify the congregation. The focus on caring for those in need is a topic that closely connects Jewish and Latter-day Saint viewpoints.

Most Latter-day Saints do not find themselves overly attracted by or fascinated with the liturgical calendars of other Christian churches, but the existence of holy days such as Passover (*Pesah*), the Day of Atonement (*Yom Kippur*), Tabernacles (*Sukkot*), and others in the Hebrew Bible likely gives Latter-day Saints an increased sense of importance and interest to the Jewish calendar. Most Latter-day Saints love to learn about how the different holy days would have appeared in ancient times and how they are practiced today, sensing that their importance for God's ancient covenant people continues to provide important—and possibly hidden—meaning for the Church.

As with other Christians, some Latter-day Saints enjoy participating in Passover meals as a way of learning about and experiencing Jewish behaviors that they believe they share through ancient ancestors and as a way of connecting with Jesus's Last Supper. Although most view these as an active and inspiring educational experience similar to studying the scriptures, they are likely not aware that these practices might be offensive to some Jews, and even more so when the Passover re-creations are Christianized. For many Christians and Latter-day Saints, ancient rituals are understood primarily as foreshadowing Christian beliefs. This view is enhanced by the New Testament description of the sacrament instituted by Jesus as a modified continuation of the ancient Passover. The reality is that the Jewish Passover meal practices of today are not exactly the same as those in Jesus's time, with many parts of the ritual added over the last two thousand years, meaning that Christian re-creations of a uniquely Jewish practice may feel particularly forced to Jews. It is important for Latter-day

---

3. Isaiah 58:6.

Saints to consider how they would feel if someone were to engage in a re-creation of one of their ordinances such as the sacrament or baptism for educational purposes. This analogy isn't perfect, of course. Many Jews do not necessarily find Passover re-creations to be offensive if they are done respectfully, with Christian themes taught separately and distinctly from the Jewish Passover practices that have developed over the centuries. But this is a potential area of both connection and of tension that should be carefully considered and explored.

Latter-day Saint temple practices exhibit much higher levels of liturgical or formalized worship than their Sunday worship services, with detailed, extended ritual behaviors designed to help Latter-day Saints experience the divine and to renew their covenantal relationships (while simpler rituals such as baptism and the sacrament are performed outside of the temple). I have written elsewhere that the covenantal movement into the presence of God symbolized by temple ordinances builds on a foundation of imagery primar-ily found on the Day of Atonement.[4] On that holy day, the high priest would progress past the veil into the Holy of Holies, symbolically standing in the presence of God on behalf of His people. In Jewish worship practice today, the *Kaddish* prayer symbolizes the movement of the worshipper into the Divine Presence and in some ways mirrors the divine ascent of the Latter-day Saint temple endowment.

Many temple practices fit better under a discussion of life cycle, but others are repeated by Latter-day Saints whenever they are able. Even with the greater level of detail found in temple practices, including sacred ritual clothing and other symbolic practices, these ordinances do not fit closely with Jewish liturgical patterns, primarily because they do not include any type of singing and because they do not coincide with a regular yearly calendar but are available whenever the worshipper desires to attend. Since temple practices are kept relatively private, they are mostly unknown out-side of Latter-day Saint circles, and an understanding of this rich area of connection between Jewish and Latter-day Saint worship is thus mostly missed. This book has pointed to a number of points of contact, such as with Jewish ritual prayer clothing, between Latter-day Saint temple and Jewish worship practices.

---

4. *Yom Kippur*; see Suggested Reading.

Dietary Laws (*Kashrut*)—Word of Wisdom

One of the areas of unique similarity between Jews and Latter-day Saints is the strong dietary codes in both traditions. The Jewish code is more involved or far-reaching than the Latter-day Saint code, particularly for those who follow the highest levels of Orthodox dietary behaviors. Numerous meats and seafoods are prohibited, and the humane treatment of animals used for food is strongly encouraged. But both dietary codes have a significant daily impact on those who follow them.

The importance that Latter-day Saints give to their health code, known as the Word of Wisdom, is demonstrated by its existence as one of the practices for which Latter-day Saints must self-report adherence in a private interview with their Church leaders in order to be given a temple recommend (permission to enter the temple and engage in temple ordinances). The existence of this question encourages high levels of Latter-day Saint observance. Although the Word of Wisdom includes encouragement to gratefully enjoy the foods which God has provided, encourages moderation in the eating of meats, and places an emphasis on vegetables and grains, the restrictions are the most recognizable aspects of the code. These include complete abstinence from alcoholic beverages, coffee, tea, tobacco, and illicit drugs. Although it is not considered an official part of the Word of Wisdom, some (but certainly not all) Latter-day Saints interpret the restriction on coffee to extend to any beverages with caffeine.

Since coffee, tea, and alcohol are some of the most frequently used social drinks in the world, this restriction serves as a consistent reminder to Latter-day Saints that they have covenanted to be different from the rest of the world. Much like with their Jewish friends, the decision to eat and drink differently than those around them serves as an easily identifiable mark of Latter-day Saint commitment and often works to reinforce rather than weaken or threaten Latter-day Saint self-identity and commitment. Adherence to this health code has also significantly contributed to a healthier lifestyle and a longer life expectancy for Latter-day Saints. Studies continue to show a life expectancy that is almost ten years longer than that of the average United States citizen. Jewish and Latter-day Saint explorations of both the specific rules of their respective dietary codes and the reasoning used for following those rules in their communities can provide fruitful ground of discovery and mutual appreciation.

The Life Cycle—Birth, *Bar/Bat Mitzvah*, Conversion, Marriage, Divorce, Death, and Mourning

As with Jewish life cycle rituals, those performed in Latter-day Saint communities also show a strong emphasis on the value of life, spiritual commitment, family relationships, and death. Latter-day Saint approaches demonstrate simpler forms than their Jewish counterparts but include important milestone markers at each stage of development that mirror those found in Jewish communities. Although they could just as easily be discussed in the section describing differences, I will present them here. They are different in detail but often show strong similarities in timing and intent to Jewish life cycle practices.

The corresponding Latter-day Saint practice that connects with the *berit milah* (*bris*) ceremony of circumcision is the priesthood ordinance known as the giving of a name and a blessing. As with the *bris* ceremony, this ordinance is either performed in the home with members of the community present or more often in a weekly sacrament meeting. Although the rite of circumcision is held eight days after the baby's birth, the name and blessing ordinance is typically performed within a few months of the birth. Male members of the extended family and close family friends are invited to come forward and form a prayer circle around the baby, with the baby supported by the right hands of the participants and the left hands placed on the shoulder of the man to the left, forming a linked circle of support for the infant in the middle of the circle. As in Judaism, the performance of this ritual connects the baby with the Latter-day Saint community. Following the Latter-day Saint ritual, the baby's name is placed on the records of the Church, although the child will not formally be considered a member through individual choice until after the ordinance of baptism.

Baptism and the ordinance of confirmation signify formal entrance into the Church by individual choice and covenant and could be seen as mirroring *bar* and *bat mitzvah* ceremonies, which signify the formal acceptance by the individual of community obligations, although these rituals occur for Jewish youth a few years later at the entrance to the teenage years (age twelve for Jewish girls and age thirteen for Jewish boys). Baptism could also be understood as similar to the ritual immersion in a *mikveh*[5] that a

---

5.   A ritual bath.

convert to Judaism undergoes, and—somewhat like the Hebrew name given to Jewish converts—Latter-day Saints believe that the new name of Christ is placed upon them as part of the ordinance. Unlike *bar* and *bat mitzvah* celebrations, which are primarily intended for those who have been born and raised as part of the Jewish community, the ordinances of baptism and confirmation are the same whether performed for someone who was raised in the Church or for someone who has been introduced to the Church later in life and desires to convert. Baptism can first be performed after a child reaches the age of eight, which is understood as the time when children first begin to be able to reason through moral decisions for themselves and when they thus begin to be accountable for those decisions before God. Similar to the *mikveh* immersion ritual for Jewish converts, which can be understood as a new birth as a member of the Jewish community, baptism is understood as a physical affirmation of a spiritual choice to follow the beliefs and way of life of the faith, and as a spiritual birth into the community and into a covenantal relationship with God. Confirmation is performed by the laying on of hands. It cements the decision to enter into the Church as a covenantal member, but more importantly it offers the gift of the Holy Ghost, the promise that God's Spirit can remain with the individual throughout her or his life if that individual continues in paths of holiness.

An additional connection with the *bar* and *bat mitzvah* rituals, occurring at roughly the same age as those rituals when children are entering into adolescence, is the movement for Latter-day Saint youth into the Young Women and Young Men organizations at the beginning of the year they turn twelve. For young men this shift signifies an important rite of passage, as they are typically ordained to priesthood office. The ordinance is performed by the laying on of hands by an individual, or, more often, by a group each holding the priesthood offices of priest or higher. The one acting as voice for the ordination also pronounces a blessing upon the recipient that gives guidance and divinely inspired encouragement. Young men begin to officiate in priesthood ordinances from this time, at first passing the emblems of the sacrament as deacons; preparing the sacrament as teachers; then beginning to bless the sacrament, ordain others to priesthood office, and officiate in baptisms after becoming priests. If consideration is given to the symbolic connection between the sacrament, which represents the atoning sacrifice of Jesus, and animal sacrifices performed in the temple anciently, then deacons and teachers correspond relatively well with the duties of the ancient

Levites (*levi'im*), while priests correspond well with those of ancient priests (*kohanim*).

Since young women are not ordained to priesthood office, the rituals connected to their transition do not include ordinances, but they are still important. Young women (as with young men) begin to lead in their organizations, being formed into presidencies that are "set apart" by priesthood blessing to these responsibilities. Although adult advisors play important roles in the organizations, the youth are those who are divinely appointed to lead and organize the activities and instruction in the groups, and youth also begin to be asked to give short messages during the main sacrament worship service. High school years also include a seminary program in which youth attend scripture classes for an hour each weekday to enhance their scriptural understanding. Although Jewish scripture study in *yeshivot* and other Jewish day schools is typically more involved and intense than Latter-day Saint seminary study, both groups show a strong dedication to both religious and secular education.

A final but important ordinance for Latter-day Saint youth (but also available to older members who have not yet received it) is the opportunity to receive a patriarchal blessing. These blessings are offered by individuals in the Church who have been ordained to the priesthood office of patriarch. They provide prophetic guidance for the life and future of the recipient, mirroring the blessings given by Israel to his posterity in Genesis 49. They are recorded by the Church and are read frequently by Church members as their own personally tailored scriptural guidance. Of equal or even greater importance than the prophetic guidance is the pronouncement in the blessing of one's lineage, designating through which tribe of Israel the covenant blessings are received (whether that designation is understood as being an adoption into that tribe or whether it is viewed as revealing a true ancestry that had been lost or forgotten up until that point). These patriarchal designations of priesthood lineage are very meaningful to Latter-day Saints and help explain some of the close and familial affinity they feel for Jews. The majority of Latter-day Saints understand themselves as connected to the tribe of Ephraim, and some believe it is their duty to help heal the ancient animosity between Judah and Ephraim.[6]

---

6. See Isaiah 11:13.

Entrance into adulthood is often marked by another series of activities with connections to Jewish life. There are some marked similarities (as well as obvious differences) between the impact of Latter-day Saint missionary service (which often begins at age eighteen for men and at age nineteen for women) and that of Israeli military service for their young adults (which often begins at age eighteen for both women and men). Preparing for a mission, being set apart as a missionary, and serving as a missionary away from home, with minimal contact with family (and with none of the typical social, occupational, or educational activities that normally characterize this time of life), have a significant impact on Latter-day Saint young adults, who often return more committed to their faith, more knowledgeable, and seasoned by service and sacrifice. Missionary service includes the need to actively discuss and present one's own faith and beliefs, to experience rudeness and rejection, to participate with others in their spiritual renewal, to lead among a group of one's peers who are all far away from home, to work effectively with adult leaders of local Latter-day Saint congregations, and to get along with companions that the missionary lives and works with for an undetermined period of time before being assigned to a new companion. All of these experiences tend to build resilience, social aptitude, and leadership abilities among Latter-day Saint young adults, much as Israeli military service can perform similar functions for Jewish young adults.

Other rites of passage into adulthood include the ordination of all prepared males to the priesthood office of elder, which offers the authority to give blessings of healing, comfort, and guidance, along with the ability to officiate in numerous other ordinances, such as the dedication of graves and the blessing and naming of babies. In many Jewish congregations, descendants of Aaron who have already had their *bar mitzvah* at the age of thirteen also perform special functions such as giving the first scripture reading at the proper time during worship services and at other times offering the priestly blessing, found in Numbers 6:23–27, while making the sign of the priestly blessing with their hands. The priestly descendants (*kohanim*) should not participate in the priestly blessing if they have drunk alcohol, if they have certain physical impairments, if they have married a wife who disqualifies them (such as a divorcee), if they have taken a life, or if they are on bad terms with anyone in the congregation. For Latter-day Saints, ordination is available to all adult males who are able to honestly and appropriately answer worthiness questions in an interview with their Church leader, including questions about moral chastity, obedience to the Church's dietary code (the

Word of Wisdom), and the faithful fulfilment of financial obligations (where applicable) to a former spouse and to their children as required by law.

Another important experience that typically occurs in adulthood is receiving the temple ordinance known as the endowment. This ordinance usually occurs just prior to missionary service or to marriage but can also be received by those who feel they are prepared for the covenant commitments it entails, which are reinforcements of the obligations incurred at baptism. The temple endowment is a lengthy ordinance (almost two hours long) that includes an overview of God's plan for His children from the creation through the Fall and onward, and a reiteration of and recommitment to the covenant relationship with God that allows His children to return to His presence. Latter-day Saints believe that modern temple ordinances build on ancient temple practices in many ways (including a baptismal font in the lowest floor of each temple that rests on the backs of twelve oxen). The endowment, in a sense, replicates the prophetic experience of entering into the presence of God, or the divine ascent of the high priest on the Day of Atonement. The ordinance is significantly more detailed and lengthy than baptism, the sacrament, or other ordinances witnessed up to that point. Because it is not openly discussed with great detail prior to receiving it and because it includes symbolism such as ceremonial clothing that has not been common for Latter-day Saints before, participating in the endowment ceremony for the first time can be powerful but also intimidating and even disconcerting. After receiving the endowment, Latter-day Saints return regularly to have the experience on behalf of their ancestors, much as with baptisms for the dead. This repetition allows them to experience the endowment again and again throughout life. Many Latter-day Saints love and feel strengthened by this repeated experience, and it helps to maintain their commitment to their faith.

Although it cannot precisely be considered a religious life cycle ritual, the Latter-day Saint commitment to receiving a strong secular (nonreligious) education in addition to their religious education parallels the remarkable Jewish attention to learning. As a well-known scriptural passage states, "The glory of God is intelligence,"[7] and Latter-day Saints believe that they have a divinely commanded duty to receive as much education as possible. Surprisingly, some studies have demonstrated that Latter-day Saints reverse

---

7.   Doctrine and Covenants 93:36.

the trend that is often witnessed of negative correlation between religiosity and educational levels. These studies suggest that, on the whole, the more educated a Latter-day Saint is, the higher levels of religious commitment they tend to demonstrate.

Marriage marks another important stage in the life cycle of many Latter-day Saints. As in many Jewish communities, marriage and family life are viewed as highly important components of a fully experienced religious life, a widespread viewpoint that can be very challenging for Latter-day Saints who are single. As with Jewish couples, Latter-day Saint courtship and engagement practices tend to follow the patterns of the societies in which they live. Marriages by any authority legally recognized by the country's government are fully accepted as binding by Latter-day Saints. These marriages, often but not always performed by a bishop in a local chapel, are considered relationships that are designed to last until death severs them. Most Latter-day Saints, however, deeply desire to be "sealed" in a temple ordinance that unites the couple beyond mortal life and into the eternities. These eternal marriages declare many of the blessings upon the head of the couple as those that God gave to Abraham, and the couple is in a sense understood as becoming a new Abraham or Sarah. Although the beautiful priestly blessing from Numbers 6:24–27 is not pronounced as it is in Jewish marriages, the blessings of the sealing ordinance express similar sentiments and contain some of the most beautiful and uplifting language in any of the Latter-day Saint ordinances. Where possible, and as determined by each couple, children are considered a crucial part and desired outcome of the marriage relationship. The duty of a mother and father is considered by Latter-day Saints to be more valuable than any other possible earthly privilege or responsibility.

Divorce is discouraged among Latter-day Saints, but it is viewed as being a necessary recourse at times according to the decision of the couple. Divorce rates among Latter-day Saint couples who do not participate in temple sealing ordinances are similar to those found in society at large. As with Jews, legal divorces are recognized as fully dissolving the legal relationship of those married either outside the temple or sealed in the temple. The sealing ordinance itself, however, is not cancelled by normal divorce processes, since it is a religious ritual performed by Church authority, not simply by government authority. This type of dissolution is known as a "cancellation of sealing" and requires permission from the highest levels of Church leadership. Although the permission is regularly granted, the process to request a cancellation of sealing emphasizes the higher level of responsibility that Latter-day Saints believe is connected to these ordinances. Although there is some challenge in tracking divorce rates for those who have been sealed in the temple, those rates appear to be significantly lower than the rates found in typical societal averages.

Rituals at the time of death among Latter-day Saints are less involved than those of most Jews (the *kevod ha-met*, *nihum avaylim*, and *shiva* mentioned above), but they are still highly important for Latter-day Saints. Although there is no prescribed period of mourning nor are there developed mourning rituals, funeral services are almost universally performed in Latter-day Saint chapels for those who have passed away. These are often relatively positive times that allow for mourning but are also considered celebrations of life that signify the Latter-day Saint assurance of a future resurrection and of the continuation of family relationships in heaven. The dedication of the grave is a prayer performed as a priesthood ordinance. Although Latter-day Saints can choose cremation if they desire or if required by their local government, burial is typically the preferred arrangement as in Judaism. As an interesting parallel to Jews who are dressed for burial in linen shrouds (*tahrikhin*) by a Jewish Holy Society (*hevra kaddisha*), Latter-day Saints who have been endowed in the temple are often buried in the ritual clothing of that ordinance and their bodies are often prepared for burial by members of the Church's female Relief Society.

All in all, Latter-day Saint life cycle rituals are designed to emphasize the importance of family, the idea of eternal progression that prepares the individual to become more and more Godlike over the course of a lifetime and beyond, and the assurance of a physical resurrection and of eternal life in the presence of God and connected to one's family. These rituals provide order, strength, and peace to the often-chaotic occurrences of mortality and strengthen Latter-day Saint engagement with their faith. Jewish life cycle rituals perform similar functions, providing order and meaning in life and emphasizing community values, respect and gratitude for life, and family strength. Much connects Jews and Latter-day Saints in this important area of religious practice.

8

Areas Where Latter-day Saint Practices Differ

By Professor Shon Hopkin

A birds-eye view of Latter-day Saint and Jewish practices reveals numerous similarities, while a closer look allows a discussion of how the practical application is expressed in widely differing ways. Unlike the belief section, I have chosen to describe many Latter-day Saint practices under the heading of similarities, since the differences appear to exist more in the application level than in the level of fundamental differences. There are, however, a few ways in which Latter-day Saint and Jewish practice are broadly different, and I will explore those in this section.

Centralized Church Organization

One of the most significant and most noticeable differences between Latter-day Saint and Jewish practice is a central organization and a worldwide Church leadership structure for Latter-day Saints. Once again, Jewish organization demonstrates a wide variety of practice across the world, from the organized but highly democratic practices of Reform Judaism to the leader-centered practices often found among the *haredi* (ultra-Orthodox).

Among Latter-day Saints, the message of the restored gospel is presented by The Church of Jesus Christ of Latter-day Saints, whose leaders are understood as prophets that help communicate God's will to His Church and to the world. The central organization of the Church presents numerous strengths and challenges. The fact that Church manuals and study guides are centrally prepared by the Church creates a noticeable unity to the message. Centralized Church authority also helps to create a similarity in worship forms and local organization across the world. Additionally, service efforts can be organized and unified much more easily when a central leadership can ask all local congregations to participate in projects with a unified vision. A visit to the Church's humanitarian center in Utah can be overwhelming, where aisles upon aisles of emergency food and supplies stand constantly ready to be sent to areas of need at a moment's notice. Latter-day Saints tend to emphasize the benefits that come from this organization, taking pride in the similarity of the gospel message across the world, the financial strength that can come from centrally controlled tithing funds that are carefully administered throughout the world, the rapidity of response to welfare needs that is possible, and the ability to mobilize far-flung congregations down to each individual member within hours.

The reality of Church organization can appear overwhelming and potentially even negative and controlling to those who are accustomed to the wide variety of Jewish behavior and thought that has developed over the course of centuries. This is even more true in an era that often exhibits strong distrust for institutions and that rejoices in the freedom of individualism in which all should be completely free to think and act without any outside controls upon their views or behaviors. Additionally, the possibility exists that centralized, top-down leadership can limit or stifle the creativity that is shaped by the needs of each local community. Strong leaders are developed in both centralized and decentralized organization styles, but the leaders in an institution with strong central leadership at times may be more trusted if they do not push too strongly against the cultural norms or culturally influenced views of the leaders above them. Some may feel challenged by this conformity or by the lack of change that they feel is necessary for the Church to remain alive and vibrant over the course of time. Of course, whether or not a single, overarching organizational system exists (as in the Church) or not (as in the wide expression of Jewish identity), communities do tend to unite and develop their own sets of values that are passed down and reinforced by participation in the community. The apparent strengths and weaknesses of the Church's central organization are experienced to a greater or lesser degree everywhere that some type of community develops. Commonly held, community reinforced values are how society perpetuates itself; although these types of community reinforcing systems can be mistrusted in others, they tend to exist for each of us in our own backyards.

Additionally, the organization of the Church demonstrates greater flexibility than might be expected by an outside observer. This flexibility is best explained through the belief in divine revelation and inspiration. First, Latter-day Saints believe that God speaks through prophets and that a God who lives and speaks will be able to help their prophets lead the Church according to the current needs in the world, rather than according to outdated traditions that are no longer relevant. Although significant changes in Church organization, practices, or policies can create a stir and even lead to departures from Church membership, members of the Church are, for the most part, prepared to accept significant changes in Church approach and policy over the course of their lifetimes. The flexibility that this potentially provides has allowed the Church to weather fairly rapid changes in which, for example, plural marriage first became an accepted practice in the Church and then was no longer permitted a short fifty years later. Differences in the ways that the Church views and responds to the role of women, to the needs of LGBTQ+ Church members and others, and to the benefits and challenges of digital technology demonstrate this flexibility. Although changes and shifts appear frustratingly slow to some, the belief in revelation does allow for change in ways that are not possible for most other conservative religious groups without creating entirely new break off churches. The reality of this understanding of prophets is that Latter-day Saints are able both to hold strongly to values (for example, in the area of complete premarital chastity) even when those values have been abandoned by much of society, and at the same time they are also able to shift the way they understand issues when they believe that God is calling them to do so.

Jewish approaches, of course, demonstrate their own methods for remaining loyal to important moral standards while also flexibly meeting current needs. Due to the cyclical nature of Jewish worship practices, time-honored messages are repeated again and again to maintain their importance in the community. Meanwhile, Jewish leaders and their communities wrestle with current challenges in an effort to approach them in ways that will follow their core ethical principles and be pleasing to God.

Next, the understanding of revelation not only strengthens a belief in the leadership of prophets but also emphasizes that each individual in the Church, including local Church leaders, mothers and fathers, and even young children have access to communicate with God and to receive instruction for how to understand the world and how to live their lives. This allows individual Latter-day Saints to seek for solutions and applications of Church teachings in ways that can benefit their unique situation, with the awareness that God can reveal truth to them that best fits their personal and local stewardships, but that He provides guidance for the entire Church through the leaders of the Church. Tension can and does exist, of course, when individuals feel that they should believe or act differently than the Church teaches. But most Latter-day Saints feel that they are able to express their individuality of thought and behavior while also maintaining their loyalty to the teachings of their prophets and of the Church. Those for whom the tension grows too high at times end up leaving the faith. Many, however, feel that God can and will guide them through these tensions, if they will be patient. In the meantime, a belief in revelation from God to prophets and the belief that all members of the Church can receive their own revelation enables a type of unity that is rare (and often viewed with suspicion) in modern, Western societies, but that also allows for the type of individuality of thought and of self-reliance that resonates with many today.

Understanding the organization of the Church can be an important exploration for Jews and Latter-day Saints in dialogue, including organizations at the head of the Church such as the Quorum of the Twelve Apostles all the way to callings in individual wards such as the bishop or the nursery leader. An important distinction between Jewish organizations and Church organization is the lay leadership that serves at almost every calling level in the Church. There are two exceptions to the general rule of Latter-day Saint volunteer leadership. First, the highest levels of leadership who are asked to leave their occupations permanently in order to serve full time receive a living stipend. Second, there are a wide variety of professionals that the Church either calls upon or employs that allow the Church to function: architects, real estate agents, accountants, and others. The remainder, however, all serve on a voluntary basis in addition to their regular occupations, from the nursery leader to the building cleaning coordinator to the bishop, who spends as much as twenty or more hours per week presiding over a ward (the Latter-day Saint name for a local congregation), to the stake president, who spends a similar amount of time presiding over a number of wards. In comparison, Jewish religious leadership consists of rabbis and cantors who are professionally trained and who serve full or part time, accompanied by other volunteer leaders in some positions and professionals who are hired to provide other roles.

The reality of lay leadership in the Church also means that there is no "trained clergy." Members of the Church often consider this a strength, believing that the sincerity, humility, and the necessity of relying upon revelation from God allow Church leaders to serve with a remarkable lack of self-interest. Along similar lines, almost all callings in the Church are temporary. A bishop will typically serve for five years and will sometimes be called by the new bishop to serve as a Primary teacher or as ward greeter the week following his release from service. Financially, of course, the lack of a need to pay the salaries for a full-time clergy also allows tithing funds to be used fully for programs, building maintenance, and in other ways. Latter-day Saints know that when they donate in the form of tithing or to humanitarian causes, that money will not be used to pay someone's salary but will entirely be used for the other purposes that were intended. Finally, the reality of lay leadership is that Latter-day Saints are trained to lead early in their lives, giving talks during worship services starting at a young age, leading their youth groups, and more. This necessity increases both the level of expertise and the level of commitment that are often found among the Latter-day Saint membership. Former President Gordon Hinckley memorably stated that every member of the Church required three things to remain fully alive and active in the faith: "a friend, a responsibility, and nurturing with 'the word of God.'"[1]

The lack of a trained clergy, of course, also can create challenges. The reality that a new bishop is called to serve approximately every five years and that the bishop's regular occupation could be anything from a plumber, to an entrepreneur, to a lawyer, to a professor means that the style of service and leadership at the head of the local congregation will vary significantly over time. Value is added as different members are required to learn the skills to lead a large organization, but leadership mistakes, some of which could potentially be serious, are likely. The absence of a full-time religious leader also has benefits and weaknesses. Members of the Church are often (but not always) more forgiving of and patient with the faults found in their

---

1.   Gordon B. Hinckley, "Converts and Young Men," *Ensign*, May 1997, 47.

local leaders, and they typically understand that those leaders cannot be at their beck and call throughout the day since the leaders have their own professions to fulfill. This can foster a strong sense of spiritual and emotional self-reliance in the Church, but heavy service requirements can also wear down the lay leadership and can be frustrating for Church members.

The practice of full-time, trained leadership such as is often found in Jewish congregations means that the religious leader typically is able to devote sufficient time to receiving important training and to caring for the congregation's needs. The members of the congregation often have a significant vote in which rabbi will lead their congregation, which can often provide a strong sense of "fit" between the leader and the members of the community.

Ordinances as Compared to Religious Ritual

Another important difference when discussing Latter-day Saint and Jewish behaviors is the way in which Latter-day Saints understand some rituals, known as ordinances. As with most religions, some religious rituals, such as manner of dress or the practice of kneeling during prayer, develop organically and naturally and are not administered or organized by the Church. Although communities within the Church will often end up speaking in similar ways, praying in similar ways, and even dressing in somewhat similar ways, these religious rituals are not considered essential.

The same flexibility does not exist for priesthood ordinances, which are understood as being performed through proper priesthood authority that has been obtained through the proper Church lines (by the laying on of hands); these ordinances should be done, to the best of the priesthood holder's ability, in the proper way. The ordinance of the sacrament, for example, has set language that should be used with exactness wherever possible. This is also true for baptism. Other ordinances, such as dedicating graves, the naming and blessing of a baby, blessings of healing, or setting someone apart to serve in a calling have a structured format that requires particular components to be expressed correctly (such as the declaration of priesthood authority) while flexibility of expression is allowed when pronouncing the remainder of the blessing.

Additionally, although an individual priesthood holder often has sufficient priesthood authority to perform an ordinance like the sacrament or baptism, officiating in the ordinance is done only under the organizing permission of a Church leader, such as a bishop. For example, although most male members have sufficient authority to baptize, they cannot baptize someone whenever or wherever they choose. The same is true for the ordinance of the sacrament. Although the sacrament can be administered in the home, a practice that allows for significant Church stability during times of isolation (such as the social isolation caused by COVID-19 in 2020), these ordinances should only be done with permission from the bishop. These institutional controls are not entirely unique to Latter-day Saints, of course; Jewish communities also only allow certain prayers to be offered when a *minyan*[2] is present, and only certain individuals are allowed to lead the community in some prayers or blessings.

Significant differences also exist in the way that Latter-day Saints view some ordinances as essential "ordinances of salvation." Some ordinances such as blessings of healing, the naming of a baby, or the dedication of a grave are viewed as helpful for the religious life and strength of the individual and community. But others are viewed as essential components of a Latter-day Saint religious life. These include baptism and confirmation, ordination to the priesthood for males, the temple endowment, and temple sealings (for those who are married). Some Jewish communities, of course, may view certain religious rituals as essential, such as ritual circumcision for males in traditional Jewish communities, but the concept of ordinances of salvation links Latter-day Saints more closely with Christian understandings such as those found in the Roman Catholic Church.

All ordinances play an important role for Latter-day Saints as they seek after holiness. In that sense, they might be equated with ancient Israelite temple practices, required by God with a significant deal of specificity, and allowing those who participate in them the opportunity to commune with God. Joseph Smith said, "Being born again comes by the Spirit of God through ordinances."[3] Elsewhere he stated, "In the ordinances [of the priesthood] the power of godliness is manifest."[4] Countless Latter-day Saints can

---

2. Typically, a group of ten men in Orthodox practice and ten worshipers in egalitarian Jewish practice.

3. Joseph Smith, "Discourse, between circa 26 June and circa 4 August 1839–A, as Reported by William Clayton," *The Joseph Smith Papers*, 24, accessed October 12, 2020, https://www.josephsmithpapers.org/paper-summary/discourse-between-circa-26-june-and-circa-4-august-1839-a-as-reported-by-william-clayton/14. Or, see *Teachings of the Prophet Joseph Smith*, 162.

4. Doctrine and Covenants 84:20.

affirm that their participation in ordinances has allowed them to feel God's touch upon their lives. Although Latter-day Saint views of ordinances may be different from Jewish religious practices, they perform similar functions.

Areas of Sensitivity

Rabbi Diamond and I have already discussed many of the areas of potential tension between Jews and Latter-day Saints, topics that require special attention and care in interfaith dialogue and in daily interactions between members of the different communities. Those that have already been discussed include the practice of baptisms for the dead, particularly in light of the fact that Latter-day Saints have sometimes used Holocaust genealogical lists in those practices; the practice of Christian/Latter-day Saint Passover (*Pesah*) meals; the critical tone in some Christian and Latter-day Saint understandings of the ancient and continued Jewish rejection of Jesus (to be discussed further below); the typical Jewish approach to Messianic Jews;[5] and the sometimes uncomfortable philo-Semitism[6] in which Latter-day Saints enthusiastically approach Jews as family members without truly taking time to understand them as full individuals. I hope that those who seek to understand their Jewish neighbors better will take special care in reading how we approach these topics throughout this book so that they can better communicate in ways that develop positive relationships.

I will mention a few other word usages and practices in which sensitivity and extra caution may be helpful. First, Latter-day Saints are deeply committed to their faith in Jesus Christ as the Savior and Son of God. Expressions of faith in Christ flow freely from the Latter-day Saint tongue, sometimes without even being consciously aware of what we are saying and the impact it may have on others. This is a central, crucial part of Latter-day Saint identity, and true interfaith dialogue should never require you to pretend to be something other than you are. At the same time, Latter-day Saints should be aware that using the title "Christ" when speaking of Jesus can feel like a direct frontal assault to some Jews. Healthy discussion in *any* relationship often spends significant time exploring similarities while approaching areas of difference with careful thought and intentionality. The frequent use of the title "Christ," however, puts the most significant area

---

5 Jews that believe in Jesus as the Messiah.
6 "Love of Jews."

of Jewish and Christian disagreement right at the center of the conversation without actually discussing it, over and over again reminding Jewish listeners that they are forever different and divided from the Christians with whom they are speaking.

Since the name "Christ" is the Greek form of the word *Messiah*, it emphasizes that Jesus is the fulfillment of the hope for a Messiah that many Jews still maintain but that they have decided does not refer to Jesus. Additionally, the title "Christ" has historically been used time and again by Christians who sought to judge, punish, and injure Jews in their communities who were typically not in positions that allowed them to be viewed or treated as equals. Although Jews are typically very good at living in societies in which they are minorities, at not taking offense needlessly when none is intended, and at understanding how strongly Christians feel about their beliefs, Latter-day Saints in dialogue with Jews would do well to act in charitable understanding and remember the long history of Christian oppression of Jews that continues to color their experience to a certain degree. Latter-day Saints have always believed and will always believe that Jesus is the Christ, but referring to Him as "Jesus" more often and using the powerful title of "Christ" with more intentionality in their conversations with Jews can only help.

The challenge with references to the name of Christ is further compounded when praying with Jews. Most Latter-day Saints feel very strongly about the importance of praying in the name of Christ and may feel that they are being unfairly forced to be disloyal to their own commitments if they do not feel free to do so. At the same time, it is important to remember that Jews and Latter-day Saints do worship the same God and can hopefully pray together comfortably. Putting the shoe on the other foot, if I as a Latter-day Saint were praying with others who directed their prayers to someone else (such as a Roman Catholic prayer directed to Mary), I would have a very difficult time feeling that I was actually part of that prayer or that I could say "amen" to that prayer, even if I agreed with most of the sentiments that had been expressed. The same challenge exists for Jews praying with Latter-day Saints. The Jewish worshipper may agree with everything that has been said in the prayer, but when the Latter-day Saint chooses to close the prayer in the name of Christ, it creates an immediate barrier and may cause the Jewish participant to feel that they are no longer part of the prayer and that they cannot say "amen."

If we truly choose to pray *together*, an activity that can be powerful in uniting peoples of different faiths, it is worthwhile exploring how to do so in the best ways possible for both sides. One suggestion that has been presented by President Dallin Oaks and others is for the Latter-day Saint who is acting as voice for the prayer to conclude, "Each of us prays in our own way, and I pray in the name of Jesus Christ, amen." This may allow all involved to feel that they can conclude in their own way while still being a full part of the act of prayer, although this approach may still be uncomfortable for many Jews for reasons discussed above. Another option that Latter-day Saints might consider is to close their prayer "in the name of God, amen," since most Latter-day Saints are comfortable with the title of "God" for Y-H-W-H, the God of the Hebrew Bible whom they equate with Jesus Christ, and that usage will allow each worshipper to think of God's identity in her or his own way. An additional option could be to close "in thy holy name, amen." This closing might be uncomfortable for some Latter-day Saints, since we typically are very clear in distinguishing that our prayers are directed to God the Father in the name of the Son. In these kinds of decisions, it is important to balance the participants' need to be loyal to their own religious faith with the need to respect each other's differing viewpoints and practices. Because it is connected to worship, prayer is a particularly fruitful and sensitive area of interfaith participation.

Three other potentially sensitive words and behaviors should be mentioned here. Readers will have noticed that both Rabbi Diamond and I have used the term "Hebrew Bible" to refer to what most Latter-day Saints call the "Old Testament." Latter-day Saint uses of "Old Testament" are usually directly connected to the wording of the King James Version. We are not trying to indicate any preference for the New Testament over the Old Testament in our use of the term, but we are simply looking for a way to distinguish the two parts of the Bible. Most Jews do not tend to be overly offended by this term, but Latter-day Saints should be aware of the historical implications connected to it. Historically and still today, many Christians view the Hebrew Bible as outdated and relatively unimportant in their efforts to understand God and God's plan for humankind. The term "Old Testament" can thus emphasize supersessionist ideas[7] that are foreign to Latter-day Saints, who tend to view the Hebrew Bible as a critical

---

7. Ideas that view God's covenants with the Jewish people as being cancelled by God.

component of their scriptural understanding and a powerful witness that helps them better understand and worship God.

Next, Latter-day Saints can ease Jewish discomfort with the names they use to speak about God. Most religious Jews believe that the name of God is represented by the four letters known as the "Tetragrammaton," Y-H-W-H (or Y-H-V-H, depending on the English spelling), and that the name represented by these four letters was only pronounced out loud by the high priest on the most holy day of the Israelite calendar, *Yom Kippur* (the Day of Atonement), while performing sacred temple rituals. Jews therefore carefully avoid the kind of use of the name of God that is common-place for non-Jews, who typically will comfortably speak the name of God either as "Yahweh" (an attempt to follow its likely ancient pronunciation) or "Jehovah" (an English version of Yahweh that is found in the King James Version and elsewhere). To remind Jews not to pronounce this name, Hebrew versions of the Bible even include vowels for *Adonai* (Lord) superimposed over the Hebrew letters Y-H-W-H whenever the name of God is found, helping the reader to not accidentally state God's name out loud. When reading these letters in the scriptures or when speaking about God out loud, most Jews will use some replacement word or name, such as: Lord, *Adonai*,[8] *Hashem*,[9] *Yod-Hey-Vav-Hey*,[10] or God. It can be painful to Jewish ears to hear God's sacred name pronounced, and Latter-day Saints can show sensitivity to their Jewish friends if they will avoid doing so. Failure to do so might be similar to the effect on a Latter-day Saint who hears someone using God's name or Jesus's name as an expletive.

Finally, if a Latter-day Saint is preparing a meal to which a Jew will be invited, it will show respect for that person's religious needs to first ask what would or would not be appropriate to serve. Different Jews follow kosher laws in somewhat different ways. The most Orthodox will only eat foods that have been prepared in a fully kosher kitchen, which will require foods to be brought in from another location. Other Jews will be able to eat foods prepared in a Latter-day Saint kitchen as long as milk and meat products are not served in the same meal. Still others will be comfortable with most options as long as no other meat besides fish is served, or for others as long as it is a vegetarian meal. At the most basic level, for most Jews who practice

---

8. "Lord" in Hebrew.
9. "The Name" in Hebrew.
10. The letters of the Tetragrammaton pronounced in Hebrew.

some level of kosher observance, no type of bacon, ham, pork, or shell-fish should ever be served. Doing so would be similar to serving a drink to Latter-day Saints but only providing coffee, tea, or alcohol as options. As a quick additional point, Latter-day Saints who will be interacting with their Jewish friends between Friday afternoon and Saturday evening should also do their best to be sensitive to the Sabbath restrictions that they desire to observe.

With all of the above suggestions, Latter-day Saints and Jews will hopefully not feel that they need to carefully tiptoe around each other, speaking in politically correct terms that could never be misunderstood or offend. Most Jews, like most Latter-day Saints, are happy to be responsible for their own unique practices and beliefs and will not easily be offended by others who may mistakenly say or do something that accidentally betrays one of these areas. Rather, an awareness of how these terms may be heard by others can simply provide space for increased discussion and understanding, and may help Latter-day Saints display charitable sensitivity (the kind of sensitivity they would hope others would show on their behalf) to certain words and topics so that the dialogue effort can avoid unnecessary pitfalls.

9

Latter-day Saint "Holy Envy" of Jewish Practices

By Professor Shon Hopkin

Although my holy envy of Jewish thought centers more on the profound theological work of individual Jewish teachers, my holy envy in the area of Jewish practice spans a wide range of Jewish behaviors. First and foremost, I rejoice in the beauty, historical richness, and joyfulness of Jewish liturgical worship. As a Latter-day Saint, I love the simplicity of the sacrament meeting in which the ordinance of the sacrament is central, lay members give heartfelt talks expressing their personal experiences with faith and doctrine, and congregational singing of dearly beloved Latter-day Saint hymns is included. At the same time, my heart rejoices in the full-bodied, energetic, musical, and rich expressions of worship experienced in Jewish *Shabbat* services and during other holy days. In times when I have attended and participated in Jewish worship services, I have felt the satisfaction that comes with learning better and better how to follow along in the prayer book, standing and sitting at the correct times, responding with the correct phrase, and listening when it is time to do so. As with Latter-day Saint hymns, familiarity may breed boredom for some or at certain times, but it also can and does create a sense of coming home and of congregational unity, and it often leads to increased levels of energy and enthusiasm as the cycle of prayers leads to an especially beloved expression of faith or a familiar melody. The beauty of cantorial singing followed by the unified response of the congregation, which in some worship places and times is accompanied by the use of tambourines or other instruments in the congregation, can uplift the soul towards the divine.

As I have worshiped in Jewish settings, a number of experiences stand out that create a sense of nostalgia for me even as an outsider. While living in Israel, I attended *Shabbat* services a number of times at a synagogue that was especially joyous in its enthusiasm to welcome in the Sabbath. The united voices would quiet reverently at appropriate times but would then enthusiastically swell to decibel levels almost equivalent to shouting without ever becoming unruly or losing the quality of worship. As the portion of the service arrived in which we would turn to the door to bow in respect for the entering of the Queen (an open door symbolizing the beginning and entrance of the sacred time of the Sabbath), the looks of true ecstasy on each face during the unified movement of bowing caused me to contemplate my own feelings about the Sabbath with a recognized need for improvement. During a *Shabbat* meal in a friend's home, I have been moved to tears as I watched father and mother lay their hands on each of their children's heads to pronounce the traditional Sabbath blessing upon them, which opens with, "May God make you like Ephraim and Manasseh" or "May God make you like Sarah, Rebecca, Rachel, and Leah."

My experiences worshipping with Jews on various holy days have created a similar sense of community, awe, and pure and simple enjoyment. I love the lessons of faith, hope, and endurance that are taught in a familial setting alongside great food and stirring music on *Pesah* (Passover). I can't easily forget the majestic blowing of the *shofar*[1] on *Rosh Hashanah*[2] and on *Yom Kippur*,[3] which cause me to feel as if angelic messengers are calling me to repentance (*teshuvah*) and to sacred worship. I have enjoyed the friendship and scriptural associations encouraged as I have assisted with the sometimes-sweaty work of building a *sukkah* (or booth) for Tabernacles (*Sukkot*), and then gathering to eat a meal there. I have stood in awe during the same holy festival in the area beside the Western Wall as I have watched the priestly

---

1. Ram's horn.
2. The New Year.
3. The Day of Atonement.

blessing, and at many other times as I have seen Jews joyfully swaying in traditional forms of prayer. To watch the happy celebrations during a *bar* or *bat mitzvah*—with the youth holding a large Torah scroll, surrounded by loving family and friends singing and playing music—is to recognize the joy of religious community and of deep respect for scripture. I haven't yet had an opportunity to engage in the nightlong study of Torah (*tikkun leyl Shavuot*) during the Feast of Weeks (*Shavuot*; known by Christians as Pentecost) that commemorates the giving of scripture at Sinai, but I have desired to join in that act of committed scripture study. I love and am deeply committed to my own Latter-day Saint worship practices, but I can and do deeply appreciate the beauty of Jewish liturgical worship.

Next, I love the energetic attention that many Jews give to the study of scripture in seminaries and *yeshivot* and homes across the world. For many Jews, the study of scripture is not characterized by a casual reading of the text or only by the kind of important devotional study that seeks for a spiritual connection while reading. Rather, one can expect an intense study of words, phrases, and themes, how they relate to each other, and how they can or should be understood in connection with Talmudic passages and other teachings of the sages. I have enjoyed the back and forth push and pull of *hevrutah* (or paired) learning, in which I have studied and discussed scripture with a partner who was willing to question, listen, share, explain, and challenge. In educational settings, most Jews are not afraid to question, to challenge, and to push hard for the best possible way of understanding things. Many Jews take their scriptural studies very, very seriously, and I admire that devotion to the sacred text.

I have mentioned my sense of awe at the persistence and continuity of Jewish faith and peoplehood throughout the centuries, and at the ways in which they contribute in all fields of endeavor in our world at large. In so many ways they have been and are a light to the world, and I hope Latter-day Saints are and will be a light to the world in similar ways. Having spent time in Israel, and acknowledging deep, persistent, and life-threatening challenges regarding the relationship of land and power between Israelis and Palestinians, it would still be difficult not to appreciate what Israelis have done with the land over the preceding decades in terms of parks, roads, archaeological exploration, improvements, and development. Having visited Jewish charitable organizations, such as Save a Child's Heart (SACH) in Tel Aviv, that serve without respect to religious affiliation or ethnicity, I am encouraged to more fully engage in as much charitable service as possible as a Latter-day Saint. I love and connect with the wry sense of self-effacing humor that I often find with my Jewish friends. Finally, even though I deeply appreciate the unity of thought and organization that often characterizes The Church of Jesus Christ of Latter-day Saints, I also have holy envy of the way that a developing understanding of Jewishness throughout history has allowed for high levels of diversity over time and across the world; I believe this adaptability has also been crucial for Jewish survival. There is much to admire and seek to emulate as Latter-day Saints get to know their Jewish neighbors better and better.

SECTION 3
Interfaith Dialogue

10

Latter-day Saint Engagement with Judaism

By Professor Shon Hopkin

Basic Themes

As will be seen, Latter-day Saint interactions and engagement with the Jewish people do not show one universally consistent approach. Some patterns, however, do clearly emerge more strongly than others, particularly the pattern of respectful friendship and assistance along with a hesitancy to engage with Jews in proselyting efforts (with some notable exceptions). The differences in approach reflect Latter-day Saint efforts to understand their own scriptural records, including statements and prophecies in the Bible, the Book of Mormon, and Doctrine and Covenants. The Book of Mormon shows a strong level of respect for the Jews as God's people for whom His covenantal promises remain in effect, encouraging others not to reject or "spurn" them,[1] but to appreciate them and their many contributions. At the same time, it also reflects a degree of judgment for the rejection of Jesus, with some of these statements strong in tone, and the book of scripture is

---

1. 3 Nephi 29:8.

designed at its core to encourage both "Jew and Gentile" to recognize that Jesus is the Messiah.

The prophecies and other statements regarding the future gathering of the Jews to their land of promise and their potential conversion to Jesus have been more challenging for Latter-day Saints to interpret regarding their relative timing. Some Church leaders have understood that the prophesied return of the Jewish people to their homeland would pave the way for eventual Christian conversion, most likely not until or after the Second Coming of Jesus. Others have interpreted some scriptural statements to indicate that conversion to Jesus was necessary prior to the divinely led return of the Jews to their land. Under the former interpretation, conversion of the Jews was mainly left in the hands of God, and Jewish–Latter-day Saint interactions remained (and remain) essentially free from any efforts at conversion. Under the latter viewpoint, the reality of the creation of the State of Israel as a secular movement without a previous conversion of many Jews to Christ prompted a belief among some that the "spiritual" return prophesied in scriptures had not yet occurred. This view encouraged some Latter-day Saint leaders towards efforts at evangelization.

History of Engagement

Latter-day Saint scholar Arnold Green has researched and published a number of excellent studies about Jewish–Latter-day Saint engagement over time. I acknowledge my reliance on his work and the work of others in this section. Some of Green's articles can be found in the "Suggested Resources" appendix.[2]

The first extended interaction between leaders of the Church and a Jewish visitor famously occurred in 1836, when Joshua Seixas was invited to Kirtland, Ohio, to teach Church leaders the Hebrew language over the course of a few months. Although there is some historical evidence that Seixas identified as a Christian in some circles, Latter-day Saints always described him as a Jew. There is no information one way or the other regarding any

---

2. See Arnold H. Green, "Jews," in *Encyclopedia of Latter-day Saint History*, Arnold K. Garr, Donald Q. Cannon, and Richard O. Cowan, eds. (Salt Lake City: Deseret Book, 2000); "Jews in LDS Thought," *BYU Studies* 34, no. 4 (1994–95): 137–64; and "Judaism," in *Encyclopedia of Mormonism*, Daniel H. Ludlow, ed., 4 vols. (New York: Macmillan Publishing, 1992), 4:1593–94.

efforts to persuade Seixas regarding Church beliefs. The interaction was highly positive for Church leaders; Joseph Smith later employed the biblical Hebrew he had acquired to explain some of his theological thinking and showed significant satisfaction at the opportunity to study with Seixas.

I have already mentioned the next important moment of engagement, when Orson Hyde was sent by Joseph Smith to Palestine in 1841 to dedicate the land for the return of the Jews. From the top of the Mount of Olives, Hyde's prayer "dedicate[d] and consecrate[d] this land . . . for the gathering together of Judah's scattered remnants." Hyde further prayed to "incline them [the Jews] to gather in upon this land" and asked God to "constitute her as a distinct people and government."[3] The prayer included only mild mention of any desire for a change in Jewish beliefs. Orson Hyde's prayer is commemorated today by the City of Jerusalem with a large Orson Hyde Memorial Garden on the Mount of Olives, which was primarily paid for by an endowment from the Church and was dedicated in 1979. A similar pattern was followed in a proclamation to the world by the Quorum of the Twelve Apostles in 1845, written by Wilford Woodruff. It encourages "the Jews among all nations . . . to return to Jerusalem." It also does not emphasize conversion, but it does proclaim that The Church of Jesus Christ of Latter-day Saints holds "the keys of the priesthood and kingdom which are soon to be restored unto them [the Jews]."[4]

In 1852, Church apostle Parley P. Pratt sounded a different note in an "Address to the Jews." "We have now shown you the door of admission into the kingdom of God, into which you would do well to enter."[5] This approach and viewpoint was shared by his brother and fellow apostle, Orson Pratt, who declared, "The main part of [the Jews] will believe while yet scattered."[6]

---

3. Orson Hyde, "History, 1838–1856, volume C-1 [2 November 1838–31 July 1842]," *The Joseph Smith Papers*, 1252, accessed October 12, 2020, https://www.josephsmithpapers.org/paper-summary/history-1838-1856-volume-c-1-2-november-1838-31-july-1842/424.

4. Wilford Woodruff, *Proclamation of the Twelve Apostles of The Church of Jesus Christ of Latter-day Saints to All the Kings of the World, to the President of the United States of America, to the Governors of the Several States, and to the Rulers and People of All Nations* (Liverpool: n.p., 1845) and appended to *Millennial Star* 6 (1845): 3.

5. Parley P. Pratt, "Proclamation to the People of the Coasts and Islands of the Pacific (Ocean), of Every Nation, Kindred, and Tongue," *Millennial Star* 14, September 18, 1852, 468.

6. Orson Pratt, *Journal of Discourses* [JD], 26 vols. (Liverpool: F. D. Richards, 1855–86), 7:187.

Brigham Young, the second prophet and the leader of the Church after Joseph Smith, would influence Latter-day Saint approaches significantly with a statement in 1866: "Let me here say a word to the Jews. We do not want you to believe our doctrine. . . . A Jew cannot now believe in Jesus Christ. . . . They cannot believe in him until his Second Coming."[7] Although Brigham Young's approach was at least partially motivated by the viewpoint that Jewish inability to accept the gospel was connected with judgments of God due to the early rejection of Jesus, the effect of his statement was to almost entirely eliminate any efforts at Jewish conversion. Two who would eventually succeed Brigham Young as leaders of the Church, John Taylor and Wilford Woodruff, worked during President Young's lifetime to soften his pronouncement of judgment but to maintain the view that Latter-day Saints should not proselyte to Jews. Together Young, Taylor, and Woodruff sent another apostle, George A. Smith, in 1872 to rededicate Jerusalem. Palestine was dedicated by Church leaders seven times between 1841 and 1933, always for the return of the Jews and never for the preaching of the gospel. A Church Mission Center was created in Haifa in 1884 but only lasted a few years. It focused on German and Armenian colonists rather than the Jewish residents there. A cemetery in Haifa still contains grave sites of early Church missionaries who died there, along with the first Church converts in the area.

In the meantime, Jewish pioneers had begun to settle in the Salt Lake Valley in approximately 1864. As nonmembers, they often were self-aligned with other nonmembers in the valley who ironically were called "Gentiles" by the Latter-day Saints. Notwithstanding this humorous designation (some cities in Utah still have a "Gentile Street" or "Gentile Way" in them), they found a safe haven in Utah, and they were not proselytized by Latter-day Saints. The Church provided meeting places for their services, donated land for a cemetery, and in 1900 donated land and money for the building of a synagogue. Utahans have elected several Jews to serve in public office, including judges, state legislators, and a governor. The 2016 United States presidential race included an independent ticket with a Latter-day Saint presidential candidate and a Jewish vice-presidential running mate.

Over the first few decades of Church history in Utah, the same theme of return without conversion was restated in the dedicatory prayers of the

---

7.   Brigham Young, "Remarks," December 23, 1866, *JD* 11:279.

Manti Temple (1888) and the Salt Lake Temple (1893). Some Latter-day Saint publications praised Zionism even while recognizing its secular character, emphasizing the role of the scattered Jewish people to bless the nations. Most of these positions lauded the Jews, but some—including statements by then-apostle Joseph Fielding Smith—continued to express themes first iterated by Brigham Young of God's judgment that required a delay in Jewish conversion until the Second Coming.

Other approaches asserted that the still-future return would primarily be made up of Jews who had already converted to Christianity. Warm, positive views of Jesus by some Reform Jews were cited as evidence of the beginning fulfillment of this reality. Church apostle B. H. Roberts served as president of the Eastern States Mission from 1922 to 1927 and noted that more than two million Jews lived in New York. By 1927 he had created pamphlets that were specifically intended for Jewish readers. These pamphlets would later be gathered into the book titled *Rasha—The Jew: A Message to all Jews*, but in 1929 Church President Heber J. Grant directed that missionary work focused on the Jews should cease. During a time when the United States and western Europe were experiencing high levels of antisemitism[8] due to potential connections between Zionism and Communist ideals, Heber J. Grant instead pushed back against the current societal view and articulated a position of Judeophilia.[9] During the Church's April 1921 general conference, he reminded his listeners of Orson Hyde's mission to Palestine and warned, "Let no Latter-day Saint be guilty of taking any part in any crusade against these people. . . . I believe in no other part of the world is there as good a feeling in the hearts of mankind towards the Jewish people as among the Latter-day Saints."[10]

The creation of the State of Israel in 1948 generated significant enthusiasm among most Latter-day Saints, with several Church leaders declaring in general conference that this event signaled the fulfillment of biblical prophecies. In 1950, then apostle (but later Church president) Ezra Taft Benson said, "In fulfillment of these ancient and modern promises [such as Orson Hyde's dedicatory prayer], a great drama is being enacted in Palestine. The Jews are returning as one of the events of the last days."[11] Elder Benson would

---

8. Anti-Jewish behaviors.
9. "Love of Jews."
10. Heber J. Grant, Conference Report, April 1921, 124.
11. As quoted in Green, "Jews in LDS Thought," 148.

eventually become a close friend of David ben Gurion, and he reported that at one point ben Gurion told him, "There are no people in the world who understand the Jews like the Mormons." Elder Benson responded, "We need to know more about the Jews, and the Jews ought to know more about the Mormons."[12] In 1976, Elder Benson delivered a discourse entitled "Message to Judah from Joseph" that emphasized the unique nature of the Church's approach to the Jews in comparison with other Christian faiths.

Elder Bruce R. McConkie at one point affirmed that the majority of Jews would not experience conversion until after the Second Coming. Whether as an adaptation or a departure from that view, Elder McConkie would later explain that the creation of the State of Israel was not the scripturally prophesied gathering of the Jews. This gathering would not fully occur until they had been converted to Christ, although the gathering to the State of Israel was part of God's "divine plan."[13] Elder McConkie's writings, along with the earlier writings of then-Church apostle Joseph Fielding Smith, combined pronouncements of Judeophilia with statements critical of their rejection of Jesus, such as those found in the writings of the Protestant scholars that they often cited in their works.

The creation of Israel also caused some Latter-day Saints to feel that the time had come to engage in missionary work with Jews. Elder LeGrand Richards wrote the book *Israel! Do You Know?* with a section entitled "New Nation of Israel Fulfills Prophecy." The book was designed to explain the gospel to Jews during the time of Elder Richards's service as mission president in the Southern States Mission. During the late 1950s Elder Richards organized "Jewish Missions" in Los Angeles, California; Salt Lake City, Utah; Ogden, Utah; San Francisco, California; Portland, Oregon; New York City; and Washington, DC some of which produced their own lesson plans. The missions were terminated by direction of Church leadership in 1959, with the directive to no longer focus missionary efforts specifically on Jews. There has not been any broad renewal of Latter-day Saint missionary focus on the Jews since that time, notwithstanding the strand of Latter-day Saint thinking that sees Christian conversion as a condition necessary before the full gathering to Israel.

---

12. Ezra Taft Benson, "A Message to Judah from Joseph," *Ensign,* December 1976, 72.
13. Bruce R. McConkie, *The Millennial Messiah* (Salt Lake City: Deseret Book, 1982), 229.

Increased enthusiasm by Church leaders in the decades immediately following the creation of the State of Israel was mirrored by numerous efforts at interfaith dialogue by Latter-day Saint scholars. These academics often downplayed statements in the Book of Mormon or by Church leaders that were critical of the Jewish rejection of Jesus and emphasized messages of prophetic interest in the Jewish return to Israel and the Latter-day Saint love of the Jews. BYU philosopher and professor Truman Madsen was a particularly active advocate for Jewish–Latter-day Saint understanding. In his publications, he often distanced the Church from traditional Christian views while emphasizing parallel themes in Jewish and Latter-day Saint thought. In 1968 Latter-day Saint sociologist Armand Mauss concluded that "Mormons [are] less likely than any other denomination to hold secular anti-Jewish notions."[14] Academic publications regarding the relationship have continued to be written up to the present that emphasize Latter-day Saint statements of appreciation and support for Jews. Some of these de-emphasize any negative statements to the degree of creating the impression that only one, unified message has ever been preached by the Church. At the same time, some writings have continued to carry forward some of the strongly critical language found in the Protestant publications that they sometimes quote. This type of language, of course, cannot only be attributed to older Protestant scholarship; as has been seen, Latter-day Saint scripture and prophetic statements have their own unique blend of the positive and the critical.

Another important strand of Latter-day Saint thinking was expressed by Elder John A. Widtsoe as early as 1933. During a trip to dedicate the Land of Israel, Elder Widtsoe befriended a Palestinian Arab who shared his own perspective on the effects of the Jewish return to Palestine. While not necessarily distancing himself from positive Latter-day Saint views regarding the Jews, Widtsoe described a broader, universalist view that included both Arabs and Jews: "The oft-asked question, 'Who are the children of Abraham?' is well-answered in light of the revealed gospel. . . . All who accept God's plan for his children on earth and who live it are the children of Abraham."[15] This message from 1933 found a home among Latter-day Saint scholars in the 1970s. A BYU professor of world religions, Spencer

---

14. Armand L. Mauss, "Mormon Semitism and Antisemitism," *Sociological Analysis* 29 (Spring 1968): 11.
15. John A. Widtsoe, "Who Are the Children of Abraham?" in *Evidences and Reconciliations* (Salt Lake City: Bookcraft, 1960), 398–400.

Palmer, emphasized that the restored gospel "is not the peculiar property of any one people, any one age, or any one nation."[16] This emphasis on the universality of the message has continued hand in hand with continued declarations of Latter-day Saint interest in the Jewish people. Church President Howard W. Hunter provided the message that has most often been used by Latter-day Saints to articulate their love for both Palestinians and Jews when he said, "Both the Jews and the Arabs are children of our Father. They are both children of promise, and as a church we do not take sides. We have love for and an interest in each. The purpose of the gospel of Jesus Christ is to bring about love, unity, and brotherhood of the highest order."[17]

Part of the reason for the continued halt placed on missionary work focused on Jews can be explained by the building of the BYU Jerusalem Center on Mount Scopus in 1989. There were significant concerns among many Israelis that the building would serve as a semi-secretive front for Church missionary efforts in Israel, and there was heavy opposition to the building in many areas of Israeli society. In order to receive permission to build the Center, the Church signed a legally binding agreement that it would not engage in any proselytizing activities in Israel, an agreement that the Church has worked very hard to fulfill over the following years. Church meetings that are held in the Center do not allow any who are not already members of the Church to attend, and Latter-day Saint visitors to the Center are instructed to not even answer questions regarding their faith to outsiders while visiting the Holy Land. In this age of high mobility and quick international travel, the Church's desire to be faithful to the agreement has created an additional degree of caution when a Jewish person desires to join the Church. In most, if not all, areas in which there are high Jewish populations, Latter-day Saint missionaries are instructed not to focus their efforts on proselyting to Jews. Further, if a Jew in these areas desires to join the Church, permission must be sought at higher levels of Church leadership. A worldwide prohibition on sharing the gospel with Jews does not necessarily exist, but the historical questions about whether or not to evangelize Jews have combined with the legal agreement in Israel to create a significant zone of caution in this area that lasts up until the present.

---

16. Spencer J. Palmer, *Mormonism-a Message for All Nations* (Provo, Utah: Brigham Young University Press, 1965), 3.
17. "Howard W. Hunter, "All Are Alike unto God," *Ensign*, June 1979, 74.

Despite these cautions in sharing the gospel with Jews, some Jews do convert to the Church. Some Jewish converts continue to emphasize their Jewish heritage, such as a group known as B'nai Shalom in the Salt Lake Valley. Herbert Rona's convert memoir, *Peace to a Jew*, provides an honest and well-written account, and Rona's descendants have continued to emphasize both their Jewishness and their loyalty to the Church.

In 2020 there were three main synagogues in Utah: Congregation Kol Ami in Salt Lake City that is affiliated with both the Conservative and the Reform movements, Temple Har Shalom in Park City that is affiliated with the Reform movement, and the Chabad Lubavitch Orthodox synagogue in Salt Lake City. Current Church leaders have continued to foster understanding, connection, and appreciation for all people, but have also shown a continued, particular interest in Judaism. Elders Jeffrey R. Holland and Quentin L. Cook have especially been involved in the development of friendships with local and national Jewish leaders. Additionally, the existence of the BYU Jerusalem Center and the increased influence of the Church in recent decades have continued to foster connections and friendships with both Church leaders and with Latter-day Saint scholars. These friendships have often begun with the work of Jews and Church members in local areas such as New York, Boston, and Southern California. The Jewish–Latter-day Saint dialogue effort led by Rabbi Diamond, myself, and others owes much of its existence to efforts by Jews and Latter-day Saints in Southern California. It is currently in its fifth year of biannual meetings (in 2020), and has included a published book about various topics of interfaith interest for Latter-day Saints and Jews, as well as an interfaith gathering in Jerusalem at which Elder Cook and Rabbi Michael Melchior, the Chief Rabbi of Norway, provided keynote addresses.

Personal Views and Approach

As a Latter-day Saint educated in Hebrew studies and in Jewish thought and literature, I have been engaged in dialogue with Jewish academics and leaders for many years. As a BYU professor committed to academic, interfaith dialogue, I am also engaged in dialogue with other religious groups, including Muslims, Evangelicals, Baptists, Catholics, and Pentecostals. In each case, my goals are not connected to conversion; rather, they stem from a desire to understand the religious beliefs of others and to help them understand my beliefs. My interest in Jewish interfaith dialogue is likely increased by Latter-day Saint views that Ephraim and Judah have a prophesied peaceful relationship in the last days, and by my religious understanding of the important, covenantal role of the Jews over time. Notwithstanding that interest, my goals in Jewish interfaith dialogue are similar to my goals in dialogue with those of other faiths. If there is a degree of self-interest in my interfaith engagement, it is that I hope to show others why Latter-day Saint beliefs may be satisfying to a rational person, with the goal of creating a better understanding and acceptance of Latter-day Saints in their communities and in the world. These goals, however, go hand in hand with a desire to accomplish the same things for other peoples with the view of creating healthier societies and building better cooperation among peoples of faith.

I must add that my efforts to understand the religious beliefs and practices of others have been deeply satisfying and edifying to me as a Latter-day Saint. The beauty of expression that I have found in Judaism and in other faiths has only increased, improved, and nuanced my own religious beliefs rather than threaten them. Interfaith dialogue can be challenging, but I have found it to be deeply rewarding. As a Latter-day Saint, I have served a proselytizing mission in which I sought to convince others of the truthfulness of the teachings of the Church, and I continue to engage in these types of missionary efforts with those who express interest among my own circle of friends; I am thrilled any time I learn that someone has chosen to join the Church. Motivated by the New Testament injunction to share the gospel throughout the world, Latter-day Saints tend to be a mission-oriented people, and I fit in with those desires. These goals, however, are not what motivate my efforts at interfaith dialogue, which I always view as a two-way conversation between equals—a deep and committed effort to understand and to be understood.

11

Jewish "Holy Envy" of Latter-day Saint Beliefs and Practices

By Rabbi Mark S. Diamond

Professor Hopkin's sections on holy envy are heartfelt reflections on the beliefs and practices he respects and appreciates in Jewish life and thought. His writing underscores one of the choice fruits of genuine interfaith dialogue: the recognition that there is spiritual truth and grandeur in the faith traditions of our neighbors. Our communities of faith have much to glean from other religious practitioners. Professor Hopkin and the editors of this series have graciously encouraged me to add closing reflections on what I most admire about The Church of Jesus Christ of Latter-day Saints.

My holy envy of the Latter-day Saint tradition is rooted in my experiences as one of the cofounders (along with Professor Hopkin and several other colleagues) of the Jewish–Latter-day Saint Academic Dialogue. From 2016 to 2023, groups of Latter-day Saint and Jewish academics and clergy have gathered at twelve conferences in this groundbreaking interfaith dialogue series. We have presented and discussed academic papers on theology and practice, prayed and preached in our respective worship services, lectured in each other's universities and seminaries, shared visits to museums and social service centers, enjoyed meals and social time together in participants' homes, and conducted public dialogues for Jewish and Latter-day Saint audiences in California, Utah, Ohio, and Israel.

Interreligious engagement is a focal point of my work as a rabbi, and the Jewish–Latter-day Saint Academic Dialogue has been the most enriching and meaningful interfaith pursuit of my career. Through this project, I have come to understand and appreciate the history of Latter-day Saints in America, especially the cycles of persecution, wandering, and redemption that have their parallels in the Jewish historical experience. Both Jews and Latter-day Saints are minority faith communities that continue to face prejudice and intolerance in America and across the globe. We have much to learn from one another about best practices to counter antisemitic and anti-Mormon bigotry.

To that end, I have enormous respect for Church elders who wisely chose to "take the high road" in responding to the *The Book of Mormon* musical phenomenon. Attendees at performances of *The Book of Mormon* opened their playbills to find Church-sponsored advertisements such as "The book is always better" and "You've seen the play, now read the book." I can well imagine what the reaction of my own Jewish community would be to a *Book of Torah* that presented Judaism in a similar fashion to the way *The Book of Mormon* depicts the Latter-day Saint Church. Jewish organizations would likely sponsor full-page advertisements in leading newspapers decrying this blatant antisemitic play, while protestors would picket theatres hosting the offensive musical. I envy the bold, deliberate actions of Latter-day Saint leaders who somehow managed to turn a negative phenomenon into a positive development for the Church and its projects and programs.

This episode reinforces a key difference between Jews and Latter-day Saints mentioned by Professor Hopkin and me earlier in this book: the diverse governance structures of our respective communities. The Jewish community is highly distributed, with decision-making vested in various arrays of professional and volunteer leaders and their supporters in Jewish institutions and organizations. I appreciate the Latter-day Saint system of governance that combines "top-down" authority, regional "flavor," [1] and local autonomy. In

---

1. I have been privileged to visit three Latter-day Saint temples in Arizona, California, and Utah prior to their dedication. I was struck by the similarities in their design as well as the differences in architecture and artwork that reflect their distinct regional and cultural backgrounds and settings.

my meetings with Church elders in Salt Lake City, presidents of Latter-day Saint stakes, and bishops of Latter-day Saint wards, I have witnessed firsthand this blend of centralized and decentralized authority. When this works well, the Church is able to harness the enormous resources of Latter-day Saints to respond in unison to national and global issues while still respecting and strengthening the separate leadership of local wards and stakes.

This governance structure is the foundation of several Latter-day Saint practices that I greatly admire: tithing of one's income to support Church programs, the essential feature of volunteerism displayed at all levels of the community, the commitment of young men and women who devote eighteen months to two years of their lives on Church-sponsored missions, and the dedication of more "seasoned" Latter-day Saint couples who devote six months to two years to missionary work. I applaud the Latter-day Saint practice in which young people help to fund their own missionary service, a striking contrast to the highly acclaimed Birthright Israel programs that send young Diaspora Jews on a free trip to the Holy Land with little to no expectation of what they will do for their home communities upon their return. I have holy envy of the Church's generous support of Brigham Young University that enables students to receive a first-class education at a fraction of the cost of comparable private universities.

In addition, I take comfort in shared norms of the Latter-day Saint and Jewish faith traditions: the centrality of the home as a primary educational vehicle and the focus of Sabbath and holiday observance, the emphasis on higher education and lifelong learning, and the principle of continuing revelation that allows Church authorities and rabbinical leaders alike to respond to an ever-changing world. In my research for a seminar presentation on the Sabbath, I was delighted to learn that Church leaders studied Jewish *Shabbat* customs and rituals as part of their campaign to revitalize Latter-day Saint Sabbath observance. Coupled with the reflections I shared above, this represents what I call "dual holy envy."

Jews and Latter-day Saints who engage in interreligious experiences and interfaith dialogue will likely come to acknowledge that they have much to learn from and with one another. This highlights the practical wisdom of an ancient maxim found in *Pirkei Avot* (Teachings of the Sages) 4:1: "Ben Zoma taught: Who is wise? One who learns from all persons, as it is written,

'From all my teachers have I gained understanding.'"[2] May we grow in wisdom through greater understanding and appreciation of the faith of our neighbors. In so doing, may we be a blessing to our fellow men and women and to our God.

---

2. Psalm 119:99.

APPENDICES

Comparison of Jewish and Latter-day Saint Beliefs and Practices

	Jewish	Latter-day Saint
God	One God created the world and is incorporeal (without body), omniscient (all knowing), and omnipotent (all powerful). Jewish images of God include a loving Father, a demanding King, the One Without End, and the Eternal Thou. Some Jews reinterpret these classical views of Jewish monotheistic thought.	There are three Beings in the Godhead, united as one in purpose and intent. They are most frequently known by the titles Heavenly Father or Elohim, Jesus Christ or Jehovah, and the Holy Ghost or Holy Spirit.
Covenant (*berit*)	The Jewish people are in a covenantal relationship with God. Life outside the Land of Israel is viewed as divinely ordained exile by some, and a mandate and blessing to serve as a light to the nations by others.	God's covenant relationship with His children began in premortality and has been reiterated through prophetic leaders throughout history. Through the descendants of Abraham, this covenant relationship will eventually be offered to all humans, who will have the opportunity to accept or reject it through individual ordinance.
Messiah (*Mashiah*)	The Messiah will be a descendant of King David sent by God to usher in the Messianic age. Some Jews affirm belief in a Messianic era but not a Messiah per se. Jews do not believe in Jesus as the Messiah.	The Messiah is Jehovah, the God of the Hebrew Bible and the Son of Heavenly Father (known as Elohim). He descended to earth as described in the New Testament and will return in a Second Coming that will usher in an era of millennial peace.

	Jewish	Latter-day Saint
This World and the World to Come (*Olam Haba*)	Jews are expected to lead lives of righteous conduct in this world. Traditionalists believe in the reward of a world to come and bodily resurrection of the dead. Others reinterpret these classical beliefs.	This life is designed to allow God's children to become more like Him, exercising faith in God and love for others to prepare them for eternal life in His presence. Through God's grace, His children will receive a glory of salvation commensurate with their desires to accept God's plan and follow Him.
People and Peoplehood	Jews are the chosen people of God in traditional thought. Some reject or reinterpret this doctrine. Peoplehood is the central feature of Jewish identity and encompasses more than religious affiliation alone. Jewish communities have a long history of taking care of their own and caring for others.	Throughout history, God has reinitiated the covenant with His people through prophetic leadership in cycles of apostasy and restoration. God has primarily worked through the descendants of Abraham to offer the covenant to all. The scattering of Israel prepared for the reidentification and gathering of Israel in the last days, primarily through ordinances found in The Church of Jesus Christ of Latter-day Saints. The Jews continue to be a significant part of God's plan for His children through the Abrahamic covenant.
Tribes, Sects, and Movements	*Ashkenazi, Sephardi,* and *Mizrahi* are three categories of Jews based on geographic origins. There are a variety of Jewish religious movements; the major ones in America are Reform, Conservative, and Orthodox. Many Jews identify as secular rather than religious.	The Church constitutes a worldwide movement with membership from a wide variety of cultural and ethnic backgrounds. For most, identity as a Latter-day Saint is mostly connected to continued participation with the religious community.

Comparison of Jewish and Latter-day Saint Beliefs and Practices

	Jewish	Latter-day Saint
Israel—Land and State	Jews have a special connection with the Land of Israel and the modern State of Israel. Zionists in Israel and the Diaspora defend and support the state and have diverse views of how best to ensure its security and bring peace to the region.	Although a wide variety of views exist regarding the actions of the State of Israel and its relationship with Palestinians, almost all Latter-day Saints support its existence and see it as a partial fulfillment of biblical prophecy and as an important gathering place for the Jewish people.
Prayer	Traditional Jews pray three times each day, with additional prayers and worship services on *Shabbat*, holy days, and holidays. There are also designated blessings and prayers for foods and special occasions.	Latter-day Saints are encouraged to engage in formal personal prayer at least each morning and evening. A prayerful attitude is encouraged at all times. Community prayer is found frequently in worship, prior to meals, and in families.
Sabbath (*Shabbat*)	*Shabbat* is a day of rest with special customs and rituals for the home and the synagogue. In Jewish tradition, *Shabbat* begins on Friday at sundown and concludes on Saturday evening.	The Sabbath is almost universally observed on Sunday. It includes worship and participation in the ordinance of the sacrament, as well as other worshipful and restful behaviors.
Holy Days	*Rosh Hashanah* and *Yom Kippur* are the two preeminent holy days in modern Jewish practice. The holy days of Passover, *Shavuot*, and *Sukkot* are important Jewish festivals with agricultural, historical, and religious significance. Each Jewish holy day has unique symbols and rituals associated with its observance.	Besides the Sabbath, Latter-day Saints do not recognize truly liturgical holy days. Biannual general conferences in early April and early October unite Latter-day Saints across the world. Stake conferences and ward conferences serve a similar function on local levels.

	Jewish	Latter-day Saint
Holidays and Commemorations	*Hanukkah* and *Purim* are two colorful and joyous postbiblical holidays. Special days on the Jewish calendar mark commemorations of key events in the Holocaust and the history of the State of Israel.	Easter and Christmas receive special attention. Pioneer Day (July 24th, when the pioneers first entered Utah) and April 6th (the date on which the Church was organized) are often remembered. For those in the United States, New Years, Thanksgiving, and July 4th may also receive attention.
Dietary Laws (*kashrut*)	Jewish dietary laws mandate avoidance of certain animal species, kosher slaughter of permitted species, and total separation of milk and meat products. There are variations in how Jews observe the laws of *kashrut* inside and outside their homes.	The Word of Wisdom guides Latter-day Saint practice. Besides encouraging the grateful use of healthy foods such as grains, vegetables, and meats (eaten sparingly), it also prohibits the use of alcohol, coffee, tea, and illicit drugs.
Life Cycle	Special Jewish rituals and customs mark life-cycle events, including birth, coming of age, conversion, marriage, divorce, and death and mourning.	Latter-day Saint ordinances mark important events such as the naming and blessing of babies, baptism (at age eight for most), ordination to priesthood office for males (during teenage years), the temple endowment (adulthood), marriage, and the dedication of graves.
Communal Governance	Jewish life is decentralized with high levels of autonomy for Jewish congregations and local Jewish communities. Ordained clergy and Jewish professionals have special roles and work together with volunteer leaders of synagogues, institutions, and organizations.	The Church demonstrates strong centralized organization and leadership (such as the Quorum of the Twelve Apostles), balanced by local leadership attuned to the needs of the community (such as bishops).

Comparison of Jewish and Latter-day Saint Beliefs and Practices

	Jewish	Latter-day Saint
Ordinances	Jews have prescribed prayers and rituals for weekdays, Sabbaths, holy days, holidays, and life cycle milestones. They are sacred acts but are not the same as priesthood ordinances or ordinances of salvation in the Latter-day Saint tradition.	Priesthood ordinances are religious rituals done through proper priesthood authority. Some are known as "saving ordinances" (including baptism and the temple endowment), with the expectation that all who wish will have the opportunity to participate in them at some point prior to judgement day.

Glossary of Jewish Terms

aliyah: "ascent" or "going up"; variously used to describe immigration to the Land of Israel and the honor of ascending the bimah (raised platform) in a synagogue to recite blessings before and after the public reading of a portion of the Torah.

am segulah: the chosen people of God; a traditional doctrine that the Jewish people were selected by God as His treasured possession with special privileges and responsibilities.

antisemitism: hostility to or prejudice against Jewish people. The thirty-one member states of the International Holocaust Remembrance Alliance, including the United States, adopted this working definition of antisemitism in 2016: "Antisemitism is a certain perception of Jews, which may be expressed as hatred toward Jews. Rhetorical and physical manifestations of antisemitism are directed toward Jewish or non-Jewish individuals and/or their property, toward Jewish community institutions and religious facilities."

Ashkenazi: Jews whose ancestry stems from German Jewish life in the fifth to thirteenth centuries. Also used to describe the beliefs, customs, and traditions of these Jews, who spread from Germany throughout Central, Western, and Eastern Europe, Russia, North America, and Israel.

Avinu malkaynu: "Our Father, our King"; a beloved prayer of the Jewish high holy days that depicts God as a loving father and a demanding king.

bar mitzvah: "subject to the commandment(s)"; thirteen years plus one day, the age of majority for Jewish boys when they become responsible for their conduct according to Jewish law. This milestone is typically marked by a ceremony in which a young man receives an aliyah, reads portions from the Torah and Prophets, leads prayers, and delivers a mini-sermon.

bat mitzvah: the female equivalent of bar mitzvah, though traditionally observed at age twelve years plus one day. In settings in which women are accorded religious rights equal to men, young women mark this milestone with rituals that are identical to bar mitzvah ceremonies.

berakha (plural berakhot): a blessing that begins with the phrase "Praised are You, Lord our God." Jews recite blessings in daily prayer services, before and after meals, and for life-cycle transitions and other special occasions.

berit: "covenant"; a sacred promise marked by religious rituals and often by a pledge that God will protect and provide for those who enter into the covenant.

berit milah: "the covenant of circumcision"; a Jewish ritual traditionally performed on the eighth day after a boy's birth.

bet din: a Jewish law court, traditionally a panel of three rabbis that rules on cases of ritual law, including conversion and divorce. In some contexts, these panels render decisions in civil proceedings between people who select a Jewish court rather than a secular court.

bimah: the raised platform in a synagogue where the Ark containing the Torah scroll(s) is found and where prayer leaders conduct worship services.

cantor: a Jewish clergy person who specializes in and leads Jewish liturgy and music in the synagogue.

cholent: a traditional Jewish stew of vegetables and meat that is prepared on Friday due to traditional restrictions on cooking on the Sabbath. Cholent cooks slowly for eighteen hours or more and is typically served as a hot dish for Shabbat lunch in observant Jewish households.

dhimmi: a designation in Islamic countries for Jews, Christians, and other monotheists who had a status that was inferior to Muslims but superior to other subjects. This status included limited rights of self-governance, worship, and religious education but also mandated distinctive types of clothing and the payment of a head tax.

Diaspora: the dispersion of a people from their homeland. In Jewish contexts, this refers to Jewish people who live outside the Land of Israel.

Ein sof: "The Endless One"; a Jewish mystical term for God.

Glossary of Jewish Terms

Elohim: a name or title used for God in the Hebrew Bible and Jewish liturgy, usually understood by Latter-day Saints as referring to Heavenly Father.

eretz Yisrael: the Land of Israel, homeland of the Jewish people.

erusin: "betrothal"; the first phase of the traditional Jewish marriage ceremony. This is also known as *kiddushin.*

etrog: citron, a special fruit similar to a lemon that is one of the Four Species used by Jews to celebrate the festival of Sukkot.

ex nihilo: "out of nothing"; a term that refers to a view of creation in which God created the world out of nothing.

galut: "exile"; the traditional Jewish belief that God expelled the Jews from the Land of Israel as a punishment for their sins.

get (plural gittin): a Jewish religious document of divorce.

haftarah: an additional scriptural selection from the Prophets read on the Sabbath and Jewish holidays after the Torah reading.

haggadah: "telling"; a collection of stories, rituals, and songs read in Jewish homes at the Passover seder.

halakhah: "the way"; a term variously used for a specific Jewish law or the entire body of Jewish laws.

hallah: braided egg-twist bread eaten by Jewish people on the Sabbath and Jewish holidays.

Hanukkah: "dedication"; the winter Jewish holiday that commemorates the rededication of the ancient Temple by the Maccabees in the second century BCE.

haredi: "one who trembles"; a term used to describe very traditional (ultra) Orthodox Jews and their beliefs and practices.

hasid (plural hasidim): "pious one(s)"; traditional Jews who follow their sect's spiritual leaders (rebbes) and stress religious piety and fervor in Jewish prayer and observance.

Haskalah: the Jewish Enlightenment; the late eighteenth- and nineteenth-century movement in which European Jews adopted new forms and expressions of Jewish identity.

hatafat dam berit: "taking a drop of covenantal blood"; the religious rite for boys and men who have been medically circumcised but did not have a Jewish ritual circumcision.

herem: a ban of excommunication, issued by Jewish religious leaders as a punishment for those whose beliefs and/or practices were considered heretical. Individuals who were subject to this ban were considered persona non grata (unwelcome persons) in closed Jewish communities.

hevra kaddisha: a "sacred society" of Jews who prepare bodies for burial and often handle funeral and burial arrangements for Jewish families.

"high church": In Christianity, churches with worship services that are characterized by significant attention to religious ritual or liturgy. Roman Catholicism, Eastern Orthodoxy, and some branches of Anglican, Lutheran, Presbyterian, and Methodist churches are often considered "high church."

high holy days: *Rosh Hashanah* (New Year) and *Yom Kippur* (Day of Atonement), the fall holy days that stress repentance and self-examination as Jews begin a new Jewish year.

hillul haShem: "desecration of the name of God"; words or deeds that dishonor God and the Jewish community. The opposite principle of kiddush haShem.

Hol Hamo'ed: "secular in the festival"; the intermediate days of Passover and Sukkot that are holidays but not days of complete rest like the beginning and closing days of the festivals.

Holy Ark: an enclosure in the synagogue that houses the Torah scroll(s). Traditionally, this is placed on the eastern wall or the wall that faces the location of the ancient Temple in Jerusalem.

holy envy: a deep appreciation of the beliefs or practices of a faith tradition other than one's own religion. This term is credited to Krister Stendahl, who served as dean of the Harvard Divinity School.

homily: a sermon or religious discourse with a spiritual message.

huppah: a covering or canopy used at Jewish wedding ceremonies.

imitatio dei: a Latin term for a theological concept of the obligation of human beings to imitate God.

kabbalah: "received tradition"; a term that usually refers to Jewish mysticism.

kaddish: "sanctification"; a prayer that divides portions of the worship service. A version of the Kaddish prayer is recited by mourners to honor their departed loved ones.

kashrut/kosher: "fit" or "proper," terms for the Jewish dietary laws and their regulations about which species are suitable to eat, how to slaughter and prepare permitted species, and not mixing milk and meat products.

kedushah: "holiness" or "sanctity"; one of the most important principles of Jewish life.

ketubah: a Jewish marriage document signed by witnesses and read during the wedding ceremony.

kevod ha-met: "honoring the deceased"; one of the two core principles of Jewish burial and mourning practices.

kiddush haShem: "sanctification of the Name"; words or deeds that honor God and the Jewish community. The opposite of hillul HaShem.

kiddushin: "betrothal"; the first phase of the traditional Jewish marriage ceremony. This is also known as erusin.

kippah (plural kippot): a small cap worn by Jewish men and some women as a sign of devotion to God.

kohen (plural kohanim): a priest in ancient Israel and someone in modern times who traces his lineage to the ancient priests.

kol nidre: "all vows"; a beloved chanted prayer that introduces the evening worship service on Yom Kippur. The entire evening service is often called by this name.

Kotel: The Western Wall, the only surviving remnant of a retaining wall of the ancient Temple in Jerusalem.

lectionary/lectionary cycle: a fixed cycle of scriptural readings read each week in synagogues throughout the world.

levi (plural levi'im): a member of the tribe of Levi who assisted priests in ancient Temple worship and someone in modern times who traces his lineage to the tribe of Levi.

liturgy/liturgical year: a format for conducting public religious worship and a worship service conducted in this manner.

"low church": In Christianity, churches with worship services that are characterized by an absence of religious ritual or liturgy or by very simplified forms of religious ritual. Many branches of Protestant Christianity are considered "low church."

lulav: a palm branch, one of the four species of plants used by Jews to celebrate the festival of Sukkot. The term is also used collectively for the myrtle, willow, and palm branches, three of the designated four species.

mashgi'ah (plural mashgihim): a Jewish religious supervisor who certifies the kosher status of products from food processing plants, markets, restaurants, and bakeries.

Mashiah: "one who is anointed"; the Messiah.

matzah: unleavened bread eaten during the Passover holiday.

megillat Esther: The Scroll (Book) of Esther read by Jews on the minor holiday of Purim.

Glossary of Jewish Terms

melaha (plural melahot): labor prohibited on Shabbat and Jewish holy days.

melekh (plural melakhim): a king in ancient Israel.

menorah: a candelabrum with seven branches first used in the ancient Temple in Jerusalem. In modern times, a candelabrum with eight branches and a special ninth branch is used to celebrate the holiday of Hanukkah.

mikveh: a Jewish ritual bath used by converts to the Jewish faith, observant Jewish women each month following their menstrual cycle, and some observant Jewish men for purification before Shabbat and holy days.

minyan: a prayer quorum of ten men in Orthodox Jewish communities or ten men and women in other Jewish denominations.

Mishnah: the first comprehensive code of Jewish rabbinic law edited in 200 CE in the Land of Israel.

mitnagdim: "opponents"; traditional Jews who opposed the early Hasidim in Eastern Europe and Russia.

mitzvah (plural mitzvot): a commandment from the Torah or rabbinic literature. There are 613 mitzvot according to Jewish tradition.

mizrah: "east"; the direction of Jerusalem and Jewish prayer in the Western world and a piece of religious art placed on the eastern wall of Jewish homes.

Mizrahi: "eastern" or "easterner"; Jews whose ancestry stems from ancient Jewish communities in the Middle East and North Africa in biblical times. They include Jews from Iraq, Iran (Persia), and Yemen.

mohel: an individual versed in religious law and medical procedures who performs ritual circumcisions in Jewish communities.

monotheism: belief in one and only one God.

nihum avaylim: "comforting mourners"; one of the two core principles of Jewish burial and mourning practices.

153

nisu'in: "nuptials"; the second phase of the traditional Jewish marriage ceremony. This is the same as kiddushin.

olam haba: "the world to come"; the Jewish idea of an afterlife.

or la-goyim: "light to the nations"; the principle that the Jewish people should serve as ethical role models for other peoples.

pareve: "neutral"; kosher foods such as fruit, vegetables, and fish that are neither meat nor dairy and may be consumed with either type of meal.

Passover: See Pesah.

Pesah (Passover): the Jewish festival of freedom, celebrated in the spring.

philo-Semitism: also known as "Judeophilia." An overt love of, interest in, and respect for Judaism or the Jewish people.

polytheism: the worship of or belief in more than one god.

Purim: "lots"; the Jewish holiday based on the Book of Esther that celebrates the victory of the Jews of Persia over their adversaries.

rav (plural rabbanim): the Hebrew term for rabbi, a teacher of Torah.

rite: a religious ceremony or act.

ritual: a religious ceremony or act performed according to a set order.

Rosh Hashanah: "Head of the Year"; the Jewish New Year that is celebrated in the fall.

Rosh Hodesh: "Head of the Month"; the first appearance of the new moon that marks the beginning of a new month on the Jewish calendar.

Sanhedrin: the ancient High Court of seventy sages that met in Jerusalem during Temple times.

Glossary of Jewish Terms

seder: "order"; the Jewish home ritual on the first night(s) of Passover featuring prayers, songs, and stories.

sefirah (sefirot): one of the ten manifestations of divine power central to Jewish mystical thought (kabbalah).

Sephardi: Jews whose ancestry stems from Spain in the eighth to fifteenth centuries. Also used to describe the beliefs, customs, and traditions of these Jews, who spread from Spain to Portugal, Turkey, the Netherlands, Greece, North Africa, North America, and Israel.

Shavuot (Pentecost): "weeks"; the Jewish festival in the late spring that celebrates the giving of the Torah.

Shekhinah: the Divine presence in the world, often described in feminine terms.

sheloshim: "thirty"; the thirty-day period of mourning following the death and burial of a loved one.

Shemini Atzeret: "The Eighth Day of Assembly"; variously considered the eighth day of the festival of Sukkot and a separate holiday in and of itself.

shemira: "watching" or "guarding"; the precept of not leaving a corpse alone from the time of death until the burial service. A shomer ("watch person") sits with the body and recites Psalms during this period.

sheva berakhot: "seven blessings"; a set of seven special nuptial blessings recited at Jewish marriage ceremonies.

shiva: "seven"; the traditional seven-day period of mourning for departed loved ones following the burial service.

shofar: a ram's horn sounded in synagogues on Rosh Hashanah and at the conclusion of the concluding service of Yom Kippur.

shohet (plural shohtim): a kosher slaughterer who is versed in the Jewish dietary laws (kashrut) of how to properly kill animals in a ritual manner.

siddur: "order"; a book of Jewish prayers for weekdays and/or the Sabbath.

simhat bat/berit bat: "the joy of a daughter" or "the covenant of a daughter"; a ceremony to welcome a newborn girl and bestow upon her a Hebrew name.

Simhat Torah: "the joy of Torah"; a Jewish holiday that falls on the ninth day of the Sukkot festival and celebrates the annual cycle of reading the Torah.

soteriology: religious doctrines, beliefs, or theology about salvation, including how one is saved and what the next life (life after death) will look like.

Sukkot (Tabernacles): "booths"; the Jewish fall harvest festival. Also used to describe the temporary booths or huts (singular "sukkah") Jews erect to celebrate the festival.

supersessionism/supersede: As the term pertains to Christianity and Judaism, the belief held by some or many Christians that Christianity does away with the covenantal promises of the Hebrew Bible. According to this view, ancient covenants are all fulfilled by faith in Christ and no longer have meaning or relevance.

tahrikhin: simple linen shrouds used as burial garments.

tallit (plural tallitot): a prayer shawl worn by Jewish men and some women in weekday, Shabbat, and holiday morning worship.

Talmud: the code of rabbinic law and lore consisting of the Mishnah and Gemara, commentaries on the Mishnah. The Jerusalem Talmud was completed around 500 CE; the more authoritative Babylonian Talmud was completed about a century later.

tashlikh: "casting off"; the colorful Rosh Hashanah ritual of symbolically casting off one's sins by casting pieces of bread into a body of water and reciting prayers and Psalms.

tefillin: phylacteries, two small black leather boxes with attached leather straps that contain verses from the Torah. These ritual symbols are worn by Jewish men and some women in weekday morning worship.

Glossary of Jewish Terms

tehiyat ha-maytim: "resurrection of the dead"; the Jewish belief that God will reunite departed souls and bodies in the end of days.

teshuvah: repentance, the central Jewish concept of the high holy days of Rosh Hashanah and Yom Kippur.

tikkun leyl Shavuot: "correction on the night of Shavuot"; a custom of remaining awake the entire night of the Shavuot holiday to study Torah and other sacred Jewish texts. Originally a Jewish mystical practice, now observed in many Jewish congregations and communities.

tikkun olam: "repair of the world"; the doctrine that human beings are God's partners in healing and repairing a broken world.

Tisha B'av: the ninth day of the Jewish month of Av; a full fast day that commemorates the destruction of the First and Second Temples in Jerusalem.

Tishrei: the seventh month of the Jewish calendar, popularly viewed as the first month due to the Rosh Hashanah holiday on the first and second days of Tishrei. In the Bible, the months of the Jewish calendar are listed in the following order: Nisan, Iyar, Sivan, Tammuz, Av, Elul, Tishrei, Cheshvan, Kislev, Tevet, Shevat, and Adar.

tzedakah: "righteous conduct"; a term that usually refers to Jewish charitable donations.

yahrzeit: a Yiddish term for the anniversary of the death of a loved one.

yarmulka: a Yiddish word for kippah, a small cap that demonstrates devotion to God.

Yeduda (plural yehudim): the ancient tribe of Judah; Yehudi is now used as the Hebrew term for a Jewish person.

yeshiva (plural yeshivot): "sitting"; a term variously used for a Jewish educational center for children, teenagers, adults, or those studying to become rabbis.

157

Y-H-W-H: the letters of the ancient sacred name of God, whose proper pronunciation was lost through the centuries. Scholars often render it Yahweh; in Christian circles it became Jehovah. Most Jews refrain from using this holy name, and instead use Adonai in sacred contexts and Hashem ("the Name") in other settings.

Yisrael: "one who perseveres with God"; Israel, a term variously used for the Jewish people, the Holy Land, and the modern State of Israel.

yizkor: "May the One who remembers . . . ," the opening words of a Jewish memorial prayer and the name of the special memorial service on Yom Kippur, Shemini Atzeret, Passover, and Shavuot.

Yom Ha-Atzma'ut: Israel's Independence Day, a modern holiday observed on the fifth day of the Jewish month of Iyar.

Yom HaShoah: Holocaust Day, a solemn day observed on the twenty-seventh day of the Jewish month of Nisan. Yom HaShoah commemorates the uprising of Jews in the Warsaw Ghetto against their Nazi oppressors.

Yom HaZikaron: Israel's Memorial Day, a solemn day observed on the fourth day of the Jewish month of Iyar, one day before Israel's Independence Day.

Yom Kippur: the Day of Atonement, the holiest day on the Jewish calendar. Yom Kippur is a full fast day observed on the tenth day of the Jewish month of Tishrei.

Yom Yerushalayim: Jerusalem Day, a modern holiday on the twenty-eighth day of Iyar that celebrates the reunification of the city of Jerusalem in June 1967.

Important Figures

(including locations of residence)

Ahad Ha'am (Asher Tzvi Hirsch Ginsberg): 1856–1927; Ukraine and Israel; "One of the people"; the pen name of Asher Tzvi Ginsberg, Jewish philosopher, essayist, and founder of cultural Zionism.

Baeck, Leo: 1873–1956; Poland, Germany, and England; rabbi, scholar, and theologian who served as leader of the German Reform Jewish community during the Nazi period.

Benson, Ezra Taft: 1899–1994; United States; Apostle 1943–1985, thirteenth President of the Church 1985-1994.

Boggs, Lilburn W.: 1796–1860; former Governor of Missouri, United States who issued *Missouri Executive Order 44*, a document known in Latter-day Saint history as the "Extermination Order" against members of the Church in the state.

Buber, Martin: 1878–1954; Austria, Germany, and Israel; Jewish philosopher and Zionist renowned for his "I-Thou" philosophy of dialogue.

Cohen, Hermann: 1842–1918; Germany; neo-Kantian philosopher who is acclaimed as the most important Jewish philosopher of the nineteenth century.

Cook, Quentin L.: 1940–; United States; Apostle 2007–.

Green, Arnold: 1940-2019; United States; Latter-day Saint historian.

Hananiah ben Tradyon: Second century; ancient Israel; Jewish sage in the third generation of Tanna'im (rabbis of the Mishnah) who was martyred by the Romans for teaching Torah.

Herzl, Theodor: 1860–1904; Austro-Hungarian empire; journalist, writer, and father of modern political Zionism who founded the Zionist Organization and organized the First Zionist Congress in Basel in 1897.

Heschel, Abraham Joshua: 1907–1972; Poland, Germany, and the United States; Jewish theologian, author, professor of Jewish mysticism, and social justice activist.

Hillel (the Elder): 110 BCE–10 CE; Babylonia and ancient Israel; Jewish leader, sage, and founder of the House of Hillel school of rabbinic discourse.

Hinckley, Gordon B.: 1910-2008; United States; Apostle 1961–1995, fifteenth President of the Church 1995-2008.

Holland, Jeffrey R.: 1940–; United States; Apostle 1994–.

Hunter, Howard W.: 1907–1995; United States; Apostle 1959-1994, fourteenth President of the Church 1994-1995.

Hyde, Orson: 1805–1878; United States; Apostle 1835–1878.

Israel ben Eliezer (Baal Shem Tov, Besht): 1698–1760; Ukraine; roving preacher, mystic, and healer who founded Hasidic Judaism.

Johanan (Yohanan) ben Zakkai: first century CE; ancient Israel; one of the most important sages and Tanna'im (rabbis of the Mishnah) in the Second Temple period.

Jose (Yose) ben Halafta: second century CE; ancient Israel; a renowned sage and Tanna quoted frequently in the Mishnah.

Joshua ben Levi: third century CE; ancient Israel; one of the most important rabbinic sages and Amora'im (rabbis of the Talmud).

Judah Halevi: 1075 (or 1086)–1141; Spain; renowned medieval Hebrew poet, philosopher, and author of the philosophical work *The Kuzari*.

Kaplan, Mordecai M.: 1881–1983; Lithuania and United States; modern rabbi, essayist, philosopher, and father of Reconstructionist Judaism.

Kushner, Harold: 1935–2023; United States; American Conservative rabbi and author of *When Bad Things Happen to Good People*.

Madsen, Truman: 1926–2009; United States; Latter-day Saint philosopher.

Maimonides, Moses (Moshe ben Maimon, Rambam): 1138–1204; Spain and Egypt; renowned medieval physician, astronomer, rabbi, philosopher, and author of major works of Jewish law and philosophy.

Mauss, Armand: 1928–2020; United States; Latter-day Saint sociologist.

McConkie, Bruce R.: 1915–1985; Apostle 1972-1985.

Melchior, Michael: 1954–; Denmark, Norway and Israel; chief rabbi of Norway, former Israeli cabinet minister and member of the Knesset (Israel's parliament), and activist proponent of interfaith and intrafaith relations.

Mendelssohn, Moses: 1729–1786; Germany; Jewish philosopher and thinker whose writings deeply influenced the Haskalah (Jewish Enlightenment).

Moses de Leon (Moshe ben Shem-Tov): 1240–1305; Spain; medieval rabbi, mystic, and reputed author of the Zohar, the foundational text of Jewish mysticism.

Nahmanides, Moses (Moshe ben Nahman, Ramban): 1194–1270; Spain and Israel; medieval physician, rabbi, biblical commentator, and mystic.

Oaks, Dallin H.: 1932–; United States; Apostle 1984–.

Palmer, Spencer: 1927–2000; United States; Latter-day Saint historian.

Pratt, Orson: 1811-1881; United States; Apostle 1835–1842 and 1843–1881.

Pratt, Parley P.: 1807-1857; United States; Apostle 1835–1857.

Richards, LeGrand: 1886–1983; United States; Apostle 1952–1983.

Roberts, B. H.: 1857–1933; England and United States; Quorum of the Seventy 1877–1933.

Rona, Herbert: 1906–1977; Germany and United States; Jewish convert to the Church.

Rubenstein, Richard: 1924–2021; United States; rabbi, educator in religion, and author of *After Auschwitz*, a work that rejects the concept of an all-powerful God in the aftermath of the Holocaust.

Saadia Gaon: 883–942; Egypt and Iraq; medieval rabbi, Gaon (head of a Babylonian Jewish academy), biblical commentator, philosopher, and founder of Judeo-Arabic literature.

Sacks, Jonathan: 1948–2020; England; former chief rabbi of the United Hebrew Congregations of the Commonwealth, theologian, and author of thirty works of theology and religious thought.

Seixas, Joshua: 1802–1874; United States; Hebrew teacher to Joseph Smith and other early Church leaders.

Simeon bar Kokhba: first and second centuries CE; ancient Israel; Jewish military leader proclaimed to be the Messiah by some rabbinic sages. Led a revolt quashed by the Roman army at Betar in 135 CE.

Simeon ben Shetah: first and second centuries CE; ancient Israel; leading Pharisaic sage and head of the Sanhedrin who is regarded as the founder of universal Jewish education along with Joshua ben Gamla.

Simeon ben Zoma: first and second centuries CE; ancient Israel; rabbinic sage, Tanna, and noted interpreter of the Torah.

Smith, George A.: 1870–1941; United States; Apostle 1903–1945, eighth President of the Church 1945–1951.

Smith, Joseph: 1805–1844; United States; first President of the Church 1830-1844.

Smith, Joseph Fielding: 1876–1972; United States; Apostle 1910-1970, tenth President of the Church 1970-1972.

Solomon ben Isaac (Shlomo ben Yitzhak, Rashi): 1040–1105; France; revered medieval rabbi and author of acclaimed commentaries on the Hebrew Bible and Talmud.

Taylor, John: 1808–1887; England and United States; Apostle 1838-1880, third President of the Church 1880–1887.

Widtsoe, John: 1872–1952; Norway and United States; Apostle 1921-1952.

Woodruff, Wilford: 1807–1898; United States; Apostle 1839–1889, fourth President of the Church 1889-1898.

Young, Brigham: 1801–1877; United States; Apostle 1835–1847, second President of the Church 1847-1877.

Zevi, Sabbatei: 1626–76; Ottoman Empire; charismatic mystic and self-proclaimed Messiah who attracted thousands to his Sabbatean movement and later converted to Islam to escape a death penalty imposed by the Sultan of the Ottoman Empire.

Suggested Readings

70/Faces Media. *My Jewish Learning.* https://www.myjewishlearning.com.

American-Israeli Cooperative Enterprise. *Jewish Virtual Library.* https://www.jewishvirtuallibrary.org.

Baldridge, Steven W., and Marilyn Rona. *Grafting In: The History of the Latter-day Saints in the Holy Land.* Murray, UT: Roylance, 1980.

Benson, Ezra Taft. "A Message to Judah from Joseph," *Ensign,* December 1976, 67–69.

Diamond, Mark S., and Andrew C. Reed, eds. *Understanding Covenants and Communities: Jews and Latter-day Saints in Dialogue.* Provo, UT: Religious Studies Center, Brigham Young University; New York: Central Conference of American Rabbis Press, 2020.

Donin, Haim Halevy. *To Be a Jew: A Guide to Jewish Observance in Contemporary Life.* New York: Basic Books, 1991.

Epperson, Steven. "Some Problems with Supersessionism in LDS Thought." *BYU Studies* 34, no. 4 (1994–95): 125–36.

Green, Arnold H. "Gathering and Election: Israelite Descent and Universalism in Mormon Discourse." *Journal of Mormon History* 25 (Spring 1999): 195–228.

———. "Jews." In *Encyclopedia of Latter-day Saint History,* edited by Arnold K. Garr, Donald Q. Cannon, and Richard O. Cowan. Salt Lake City: Deseret Book, 2000.

———. "Jews in LDS Thought." *BYU Studies* 34, no. 4 (1994–95): 137–64.

———. "Judaism." *Encyclopedia of Mormonism.* Edited by Daniel H. Ludlow. 4 vols. New York: Macmillan Publishing, 1992. 4:1593–94.

Gordis, Daniel. *Israel: A Concise History of a Nation Reborn.* New York: Ecco, 2017.

Heschel, Abraham Joshua. *The Sabbath: Its Meaning for Modern Man.* New York: Farrar Straus & Giroux, 2005.

Hyde, Orson. "Prayer of Orson Hyde on the Mount of Olives." In *Orson Hyde to Orson Pratt, 2 November 1841, Alexandria, Egypt.* Reprinted in *Joseph Smith Jr. History of The Church of Jesus Christ of Latter-day Saints.* Edited by B. H. Roberts. 7 vols. Salt Lake City: Deseret News, 1908. 4:456–57.

Jacobs, Louis. *The Book of Jewish Belief.* Springfield, NJ: Behrman House, 1984.

Jacobs, Louis. *The Book of Jewish Practice.* Springfield, NJ: Behrman House, 1987.

Madsen, Truman G., ed. *Reflections on Mormonism: Judaeo-Christian Parallels.* Provo, UT: Religious Studies Center, Brigham Young University, 1978.

Mauss, Armand L. "Mormon Semitism and Anti-Semitism." *Sociological Analysis* 29 (Spring 1968): 7–19.

Millet, Robert L., and Shon D. Hopkin. *Mormonism: A Guide for the Perplexed.* London: Bloomsbury Publishing, 2015.

Pew Research Center. "A Portrait of Jewish Americans." Updated October 1, 2013. https://www.pewforum.org/2013/10/01/jewish-american-beliefs-attitudes-culture-survey/.

Peli, Pinchas H. *Shabbat Shalom: A Renewed Encounter with the Sabbath.* Washington, DC: B'nai B'rith Books, 1988.

Potok, Chaim. *Wanderings: Chaim Potok's History of the Jews.* New York: Ballantine Books, 1978.

Rosenstein, Marc J. Turning Points in *Jewish History.* Philadelphia: The Jewish Publication Society, 2018.

Tanakh—The Holy Scriptures, The New JPS Translation according to the Traditional Hebrew Text. Philadelphia: Jewish Publication Society, 1988.

Telushkin, Joseph. *Jewish Literacy.* New York: William Morrow, 2008.

Underwood, Grant. "The Jews and Their Future in Early LDS Doctrine." *BYU Studies* 34, no. 4 (1994–95): 111–24.

Welch, John W. "Three Views on Latter-day Saints and the Jews." *BYU Studies* 34, no. 4 (1994–95): 109–10.

Wiesel, Elie. *Night.* New York: Hill and Wang, 2006.

About the Authors

Rabbi Mark S. Diamond

Mark S. Diamond was born in Chicago and grew up in a southern suburb, Park Forest. He earned a bachelor's degree in liberal arts from Carleton College in Northfield, Minnesota, and a master of arts in Jewish studies, rabbinical ordination, and an honorary doctorate of divinity from the Jewish Theological Seminary in New York. He completed postgraduate studies at Jerusalem's Shalom Hartman Institute, a pluralistic center of higher learning and one of Israel's leading think tanks.

He has served as a rabbi of Conservative Jewish congregations, executive vice president of the Board of Rabbis of Southern California, and director of the Los Angeles region of the American Jewish Committee. Currently, he is a senior lecturer in Jewish Studies at Loyola Marymount University (LMU) in Los Angeles, where he teaches core curriculum courses in interreligious studies, Jewish thought, and Israel studies. In addition, he is a professor of Practical Rabbinics at the Academy for Jewish Religion California (AJRCA), Los Angeles.

He has participated in a wide variety of interfaith projects, including Catholic–Jewish, Protestant–Jewish, evangelical Christian–Jewish, and Muslim–Jewish dialogues.

Mark has been married to his wonderful wife, Lois, for more than four decades. They have three grown children—Adina, Ariella, and Jeremy—as well as a son-in-law, Jason; a daughter-in-law, Sara; and three adorable and active grandchildren—Matthew, Maya, and Samantha. He is grateful to them for their abiding love and support.

Professor Shon Hopkin

Shon Hopkin grew up in Ft. Worth, Texas. He received a bachelor's degree in Ancient Near Eastern studies with an emphasis in biblical Hebrew at Brigham Young University and a master's degree in the same subject, with an emphasis in Arabic. In the middle of his undergraduate studies, he served a mission in northern Spain. His experience with Spanish, Hebrew, and Arabic pointed him to doctoral studies at the University of Texas in Austin that focused primarily on medieval Jewish, Muslim, and Christian literature from the Iberian peninsula. These different areas of focus also led to many months studying abroad primarily in Israel, Syria, and Turkey.

Shon is currently an associate professor of Ancient Scripture in Religious Education at Brigham Young University. He has served on the Religious Outreach Council at BYU since it was formed, most recently serving as its chair, engaging in interfaith dialogue efforts with Evangelical, Pentecostal, Muslim, and Jewish academics and religious leaders. During that service, he met Rabbi Diamond while he was visiting BYU. They quickly learned of each other's interest in interfaith work, which led to a warm friendship and a plan to cooperate in the Jewish–Latter-day Saint Academic Dialogue project. His dialogue experiences with Rabbi Diamond and many others from the Jewish community have been some of the warmest academic and religious experiences of his life.

Shon and his wife, Jennifer, have been married for twenty-five years and currently live in Orem, Utah. They have four children, Connor, Makaeli, Bryn, and Ethan—along with a daughter-in-law, Katy (married to Connor), and two grandchildren, Bennett and Brielle. His family relationships, along with his religious convictions and associations, are the source of his greatest joy.

Scan the QR code to purchase
and see other books in the
Understanding Our Neighbors Series